FINDING YOUR CALM SPACE

Thirty-One Ways to Find Calm in a Crazy World

Karen Lawrence

Copyright © 2020 Karen Lawrence

All rights reserved

No part of this book may be reproduced, or stored in a retrieval system, or transmitted in any form or by any means, electronic, mechanical, photocopying, recording, or otherwise, without express written permission of the publisher.

ISBN-13: 9798567743454

Cover design by: Karen Lawrence

For all my wonderful Yoga students who have inspired me to write this book

CONTENTS

Title Page
Copyright
Dedication
Introduction
Why We Need Calm   1
Day One: Sitting Still   3
Day Two: Calming the Nervous System   7
Body   13
Day Three: Body Scan   14
Day Four: Walking Barefoot   18
Day Five: Restorative Yoga   23
Day Six: Nourishing Food   29
Day Seven: Secure and Loving Touch   34
Day Eight: Turning Upside Down   40
Day Nine: Calming Essential Oils   45
Day Ten: Cool Water   50
Breath   55
Day Eleven: Breath Awareness   56

Day Twelve: Belly Breathing	62
Day Thirteen: Alternate Nostril Breathing	66
Day Fourteen: Ocean Breath	71
Day Fifteen: Chanting and Singing	76
Nature	81
Day Sixteen: Walking Outdoors	82
Day Seventeen: Nature Meditation	87
Day Eighteen: Engaging with Nature	92
Day Nineteen: Listening Meditation	97
Creativity	103
Day Twenty: Baking Bread	104
Day Twenty-One: Journaling for Calm	109
Day Twenty-Two: Crafting and Creativity	116
Day Twenty-Three: Haiku	122
Connection	127
Day Twenty-Four: Gratitude	128
Day Twenty-Five: Loving Kindness	133
Day Twenty-Six: Mantra Meditation	141
Day Twenty-Seven: Yoga Nidra	146
Building Calm Into Your Life	153
Day Twenty-Eight: Sacred Space	154
Day Twenty-Nine: Reflection	160
Day Thirty: Calm First Aid	165
Day Thirty-One: Making Time for Calm	170
Thank you for joining me for these thirty-one days of calm.	176

Links and Further Reading	178
About The Author	191

INTRODUCTION

Life is stressful. Especially these days. Mental health statistics are soaring. Inflammatory disease is on the increase. Everyone needs calm in a crazy world. This little book offers you thirty-one simple ways to find calm space for wellbeing, health and happiness. It is designed to be read over one month, discovering a new calm practice each day.

Most of the calm practices in this book can be done in just ten minutes. Each practice is explained in easy steps. They are designed to be accessible no matter what your age, background or resources.

There are plenty of ways to find calm space. Together we will explore calm practices focusing on the body, the breath, the natural world, creativity and connection. We will conclude with some inspiring ideas about building regular and reliable calm into your life.

I am a busy mum of seven. I have worked as a midwife, a tax inspector, a yoga teacher and a reflexologist. All these experiences have taught me why we need calm and how to find it. This book aims to share what I have learned.

I believe you are more likely to try a calm practice if you understand something about why it works. I explain how your body and brain respond to calming practices and why these activities can make a lasting difference to your life.

I have included links to further reading and more ways to develop your favourite calm practices. You can find these at the end of this book.

Everyone has difficult stuff in their lives. Maybe you have a tough job, health or money worries or tricky relationships. Perhaps you just struggle with anxiety for no obvious reason. Often it seems as if the world has gone crazy. I can't make that stuff go away. I only wish I could. Instead I offer you this little book to help you find ways to cope better and feel better. Everyone needs a calm space nowadays. It's time to find your calm space.

WHY WE NEED CALM

DAY ONE: SITTING STILL

Sitting in the kitchen sipping coffee one morning, I told my husband I was writing a book about calm. He gave me a long thoughtful look. Then he spoke carefully - the way you speak to someone who might easily explode. 'Well', he said, 'I can think of quite a lot of people who seem calmer than you.'

He's right. I am not a very calm person. My family will tell you that I easily lose my temper, often at small things. Plenty of things upset me. I am not a paragon of patience. I have not achieved any sort of buddha-like state. Am I qualified to be writing this at all?

The only reason I can write about finding calm is that I need calm myself. Every single day. The stresses of my life - being mum to a big family, having a disabled child, running a small business - make me ravenous for peace. Finding daily calm is essential to my survival in this crazy world.

My quest for calm has led me on a journey. Along my way I have discovered slow Yoga, meditation, the benefits of nature, Reflexology, gratitude practices and more. Over the last few years I have been sharing some of this toolkit my Yoga and Reflexology clients. This book aims to share more widely some of what I have learned about finding calm.

What Happens When I Don't Make Space for Calm

When I don't make space for calm, things go wrong. I break things, shout at my children and feel miserable. Unexpected problems send me into a tailspin of angry tears. I catch colds, I make more mistakes, I forget things. Usually the people who suffer most are my family and closest friends. Finding calm is something I owe to myself, my loved ones and the wider community.

Life in a Crazy World

Everyone has difficult stuff in their lives. Maybe you have a tough job, health or money worries or tricky relationships. Perhaps you just struggle with anxiety for no obvious reason. Often it seems as if the world has gone crazy. I can't make that stuff go away, but I hope this little book will help you find ways to cope better. Everyone needs a calm space nowadays.

Daily Calm Practices

This book suggests one simple calm practice for you to try you each day, for 31 days. All the practices aim to be accessible and flexible. Most of them will take up no more than five to thirty minutes of your busy day.

Almost certainly you will enjoy some of these practices more than others. That's fine. The whole idea is to give you a menu of calming ideas. You can choose your favourites to repeat regularly. You are welcome to discard the ones that don't suit you for now. Perhaps one day you will revisit some of them. You may also have other brilliant calming things to do which I don't talk about. That's fantastic. Please keep doing them. But why not try a few new suggestions too?

Sit for Five Minutes

Often the simple ways are the best. Sitting quietly for just five minutes is a lovely way to find calm. And anyone can do it. I have particular places where I like to sit - a corner of my garden for warm days, a comfy chair facing a picture of a beach for rainy ones. I put my phone down, maybe light a candle, and just sit. No agenda. No right or wrong way to do it. Simply stopping and sitting still creates a calm space in your day.

Timers

Setting a timer can help you relax. You don't need to worry about being late for whatever you need to do next. This is your calm space. Choose a gentle and soothing alarm sound so you are not jolted fiercely from your relaxation. Some people like to use meditation or focus apps which play soothing sounds or plant trees in virtual forests.

Today's Calm Practice: Sitting Still

Find somewhere you can sit still for five or ten minutes, preferably without being disturbed. You can sit on a chair, on a cushion on the floor or outside on the grass if it's a nice day. Make sure you are comfortable. Cosy blankets and soft cushions are positively encouraged. Bring a nice cup of coffee or tea if you like. Relax. Set a timer for five or ten minutes. No need to be heroic and sit for longer. Sit. Notice what thoughts go through your mind. Don't try to stop them. Just sit and relax. Notice how you feel when the time is up.

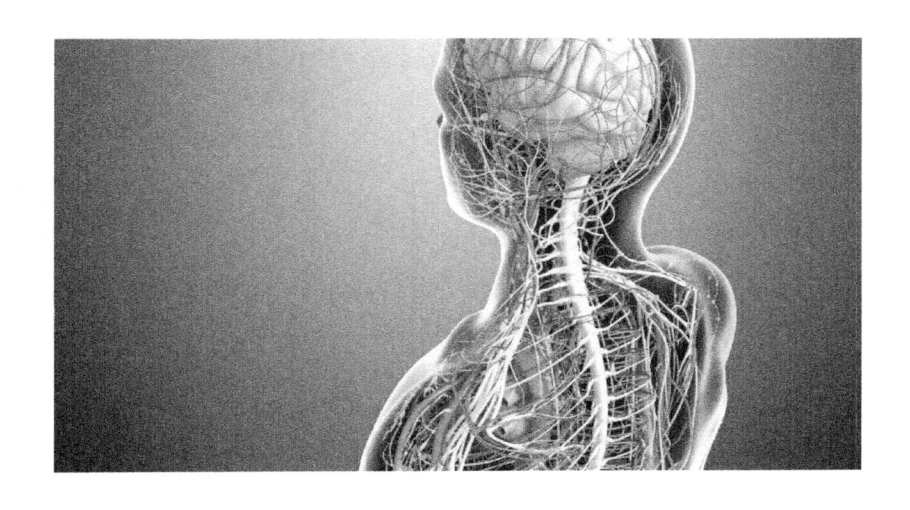

DAY TWO: CALMING THE NERVOUS SYSTEM

I have trained as a midwife, a health visitor, a yoga teacher and a reflexologist. During my studies for all these professions I learned about the nervous system. My nerves tell my arm to move or whether my tea is too hot to drink. But there is much more. My amazing nervous system regulates all the different processes of my mind and body. This means my thoughts, emotions and body are not separate, but intimately interconnected. Understanding my nervous system helps me understand how to find calm.

Keeping it Simple

I am going to talk about science and use some long words. I promise to keep it simple. A little knowledge about calm and the nervous system can motivate you to develop regular calm practices. Meditation, breathing practices and all the rest aren't just woo. We know from science that they have real and measurable effects on our mental and physical wellbeing.

Autonomic Nervous System

Your nervous system is the super-complicated way your body coordinates everything that goes on inside you. The **somatic nervous system** which is the one you use when you decide to move your arm to pick up that cup of tea. It controls voluntary movements. The **autonomic nervous system** isn't under your direct conscious control. It tells your organs and internal processes what to do from moment to moment to keep you alive.

You also have an **enteric nervous system**, which controls your gastrointestinal system. This may be involved when we talk about having a gut feeling about something. The key point about the autonomic and enteric nervous systems is that you can't control them directly, but they determine how you feel and function. The good news is that there are lots of ways you can influence them indirectly. This means you help yourself feel better.

Sympathetic and Parasympathetic Nervous System

Lets zoom in on the autonomic nervous system - the one that controls all your organs. This system dates all the way back to our reptilian ancestors. The autonomic system is controlled by your hypothalamus in your brain and by hormones or neurotransmitters. It has two main branches, called the **sympathetic nervous system** and the **parasympathetic nervous system.**

The **sympathetic nervous system** is in charge of the **'fight or flight'** response. When your body senses danger, challenge or threat, the sympathetic nervous system takes charge. Stimulated by hormones like adrenaline or norepinephrine, it tells your heart to beat faster, your blood to clot more readily, your brain to be on full alert, your liver to metabolise glucose and your skin to sweat. It is getting you into the best possible state to survive an attack. If a wild animal gores you, you will bleed less. If you have a chance to run away, you will run faster. You will think quickly and fight with focus.

Now let's look at the other branch of the autonomic nervous system, the **parasympathetic nervous system**. Activities like yoga, meditation, massage and spending time in nature all help wake up the parasympathetic system. It is often called the **'rest and digest'** response. In this state your breathing and heart rate slows. Your blood pressure is lowered. Your digestive system gets to work, and the creative right hemisphere of your brain takes charge. You feel calm and maybe a bit sleepy. Your body gets the opportunity to repair damage to cells and organs. A sense of connection and warmth predisposes you towards positive and loving relationships with others. The body and the emotions are in a healing state of rest. You are in your calm space.

Balance is Key

Our wellbeing depends on getting the right balance between the sympathetic and parasympathetic states. If we are always calm and sleepy, we may become bored, sluggish and depressed. But excessive excitement and over stimulation without opportunities for rest and recovery will make us ill and eventually kill us. In modern life many people live on constant alert. Some stress is good for us, but excessive and uncontrolled stress is toxic.

The effects of stress are cumulative. Unrelieved stress weakens the immune system, making us more likely to catch infectious diseases. It also makes us more prone to heart disease, stomach ulcers, cancers and serious mental health problems. Stress without rest is seriously bad news. This is why we absolutely need calm on a daily basis.

Calm Practices

We all have stress in our lives, but there are lots of ways we can learn to get into that restful parasympathetic state. The calm practices in this book are designed to help you enter the parasympathetic "rest and digest" state. By deliberately introducing simple calming activities into your daily life, you can help balance your nervous system, improve the health and function of your body, and feel better.

The Vagus Nerve

You might have heard people talk about the vagus nerve. This big nerve contains eighty per cent of all the parasympathetic nerve fibres in the body. Activating the vagus nerve helps us get into that lovely calm state. The vagus nerve has two branches. It runs from the brainstem down through the neck and chest to the gut. It influences your heart rate and digestion, as well as your immune system. Scientists are discovering lots of evidence that activating the vagus nerve can help with all sorts of major health problems such as post-traumatic stress disorder and inflammatory bowel disease.

Today's Calm Practice: Rest with an Eye Pillow

One easy way to activate the vagus nerve is through gentle pressure around the eye sockets. That is why children (and adults) instinctively rub their eyes when they are getting ready for sleep. Resting with a gentle weight over the eyes helps you get into a relaxed, parasympathetic state.

Today find ten minutes when you can lie down undisturbed in a quiet place. If you have an eye pillow - a small cushion filled with rice or something similar - settle this over your eyes. If you don't have an eye pillow, try using a small folded towel over your eyes, or alternatively lie facing downwards with a cushion under your forehead. You might also like to give yourself a gentle massage around the outside of your eyes with clean fingertips. Take care not to touch your eyes or lashes.

Put some relaxing music on if you like. Close your eyes and rest quietly. Set a timer for ten minutes, or stay longer if you have time. The soothing weight of the eye pillow will slow your breathing and heart rate so you feel calm and relaxed.

When the timer sounds, take time to stretch and begin to move slowly. Notice how you feel now.

BODY

DAY THREE: BODY SCAN

When I was nine years old, a slightly hippieish teacher used to come to my primary school to teach drama. At the end of every session she would get us to lie down on the slightly smelly floor of the school hall. We all had to lie still and close our eyes. Then she would talk us through a simple body scan relaxation. I can't remember anything about the rest of the drama classes, but I will never forget the lovely feeling of calm that washed over me as I lay on my back, eyes shut. Listening to her guiding voice, I took a mental journey around my body and relaxed completely. That was my first experience of a body scan meditation.

I also recall that this teacher called us collectively 'people' instead of 'children'. She really was quite alternative for a 1970s village primary school!

Where do you feel it in your body?

Fast forward forty-five-plus years, and I remain utterly convinced of the calming power of the simple body scan. Meditating on the body is an ancient practice. It is always available. When I focus on the body I travel inward. I enter the here and now. I loosen ties to outward concerns. I become present to myself. My mind is focused and soothed. I rest in the wonder of my own physical being.

The body, mind and emotions are all intimately connected. A body scan takes me out of my preoccupied thoughts and into my present experience. It is a quick and easy path to calm relaxation.

Body Image and Judgement

Many people have negative thoughts about their bodies. Beautiful models confess to body anxiety and eating disorders. Few of us are completely satisfied with our body shape or appearance. A body scan meditation should never be about judgement. It is not about appearance, although we may inevitably notice markers of health. It is an inner journey of loving self-respect. I notice and honour all the parts of my body with my attention. Sometimes I like to thank each body part in turn. I thank my toes for enabling me to balance. I thank my thighs for strong muscles to walk. I thank my belly for digesting my food to give me energy.

Imperfect as it is, my body does remarkable things for me all the time. It keeps me alive and active. It gives me daily opportunities to do good in the world. I love my body exactly as it is today.

Today's Calm Practice: Body Scan Relaxation

A body scan relaxation can help you feel calm at any time. Today's short exercise is to rest and pay attention to your body. Here's how to do it.

Find a quiet place to sit or lie down for ten to fifteen minutes. If you only have limited time in your busy day, set a timer before you begin. This means you don't have to worry about the time.

Lie down on your back on the floor if you can. You can lie on a mat or rug, or even outdoors on grass or sand. It's better not to lie on your bed as you might just fall asleep! You can lie on your belly or side if you prefer. Alternatively sit on an upright chair with your feet planted on the floor.

Take some time to make sure you are comfortable. You might like a small pillow under your head, a support under your knee or a blanket on top to keep you cosy. If you are sitting, make sure your lower back is supported. Your seat should be high enough that your knees are lower than your hips. Sit on a cushion if you need to.

Take two or three long, slow breaths. Then close your eyes.

Consciously relax your shoulders and your jaw.

Feel what you are sitting or lying on. Feel the ground underneath you. Become aware of the space around you - below, above and on each side.

Bring your attention to your body. Begin at the top of your head and start to travel slowly downwards.

Taking each part of your body in turn, notice how it feels. Acknowledge each part of your body as your mind scans downwards, from the crown of your head down to your face, neck, shoulders, and so on.

Keep scanning downwards, slowly and steadily. Notice how each part of your body feels right now.

Try not to think of feelings as good or bad. Some parts of you might feel tight or achey. Other parts might feel fine. Don't try to change anything. Simply pay attention.

If you wish, say thank you to each part of your body as you acknowledge it.

If you find it difficult to slow your mind down enough to notice how the body feels, you can try tensing and relaxing each part of the body in turn. This helps bring more focus to that area.

Keep on scanning down like this until you get all the way to your toes.

Now simply rest and relax. Lie or sit for a few minutes more if you can. Notice how you feel now.

When you are ready, get up slowly and get on with your day.

DAY FOUR: WALKING BAREFOOT

I love beaches. I love sand and shingle and rocks. Walking barefoot along a beach rests my heart and lifts my soul. It is one of my favourite things to do in the world.

When I was a little girl, my Dad used to tell me that

anyone who was born in Brighton has an innate ability to walk barefoot on a pebbly beach without pain. My Dad and I were both born in Brighton. He passed away years ago, but to this day I remember him and smile whenever I am picking my uncomfortable way across shingle in bare feet. I tell myself it is true, and feel special. I am a child of the beach. I belong here.

The soles of our feet can tread a pathway to calm.

Holy Ground

Many faiths and traditions share a deep sense that the ground is holy. Native Americans and many indigenous peoples believe that Mother Earth is a sacred, living being. Walking barefoot connects us directly to the energy of the earth.

In India and the Middle East, worshippers in mosques, churches and synagogues remove their shoes before entering a sacred space to pray. This is connected with ideas of cleanliness and purity. In the Bible, God tells Moses to take off his shoes in the Divine presence because he is standing on holy ground.

Honouring a Sacred Space

There is something special about walking barefoot in a favourite place. The soles of your feet connect with the damp grass in your garden at dawn. You imprint the sand on a quiet beach. Some people like to walk around the boundaries of a significant space. As animals mark territory, so we enhance our sense of security by honouring a place we belong. Our ancestors valued their connection to the earth. We can benefit from doing the same.

Feeling Free

Some schools of Yoga insist that practice must always be barefoot, to ensure a balanced sense of connection. I love practising Sun Salutations on the lawn in bare feet. The cool of the dew in early morning is so refreshing.

Taking off my shoes makes me feel free. That barefoot feeling connects me to my inner child. She laughs and comes out to play. Footwear subtly symbolises all the constraints of our modern lives and daily commitments. Sometimes removing your shoes and socks and wriggling your toes in mud or grass is enough to create a complete sense of liberation.

Feet are Amazing

Your feet are remarkable. One quarter of all your bones are in your feet. Together with a complex network of tendons, muscles and ligaments, these bones allow you to walk, run and dance with stability and balance. Your feet adapt to rough, uneven or slippery surfaces to keep you upright and safe. If the bones in your feet are out of alignment, the rest of the body will suffer. Each foot has 250,000 sweat glands and over 14,000 nerve endings. Any damage to the nerve endings in the feet can have serious consequences. Feet are incredibly sensitive. They are your primary connection to the earth.

Walking Barefoot for Health

Walking barefoot has many health benefits. There is growing evidence, both anecdotal and from scientific studies, that regular barefoot walking is good for you. It can help with chronic pain and inflammation. Walking barefoot can improve sleep, strengthen the immune system, reduce anxiety. It has also been shown to prevent period pains and hormonal imbalances as well as improving energy levels. A simple barefoot walk on grass, sand or earth makes you feel better and calmer.

Many people believe that direct barefoot connection to the earth can connect you to the earth's free electrons and stabilise many body systems. This is often described as "grounding". You can read more about the research and thinking behind this in the links for further reading.

Better Foot Health - and Injuries?

Walking barefoot can strengthen the bones and arches in your feet, as well as giving your lower leg muscles a good workout. However there is much debate about walking substantial distances or running barefoot. Some people swear by barefoot running, but it can also cause injuries. Plantar fasciitis, ankle and calf injuries have all been implicated, especially when people try to run too far too quickly in bare feet.

I recommend walking only short distances barefoot, and on safe surfaces. Avoid walking barefoot if you have any foot injuries or damage to the nerves in your feet or lower legs. Always inspect your feet and wash them after a barefoot experience. We have shoes for good reasons, and we should be grateful for them!

Foot Massage and Reflexology

Reflexology is a very safe way to get amazing health benefits via your feet. Humans have been massaging one another's feet for health and relaxation for millennia. Feet are intimately connected to the wellbeing of the entire body and mind. As a practising Reflexologist and enthusiastic Reflexology client, I know that Reflexology provides all the same benefits as barefoot walking in a super-concentrated form. Massage and stimulation of the reflex points on the feet is one of the most reliable ways to relax into the parasympathetic state of calm.

Reflexology has been shown to help with many health problems, especially those connected with stress, inflammation and over-stimulation of the body's systems. There are some remarkable stories of full recovery. Virtually every client reports improvements in mood and wellbeing. Reflexology and foot massage is restful and healing for the whole person.

Today's Calm Practice: Barefoot Walking

For today's calm practice, take off your shoes and socks and feel the ground under your feet. If possible, take a short barefoot walk around your garden, or in a park or on a beach. Make sure you are safe and comfortable.

Walk slowly and feel all the sensations under your soles. Imagine the pattern of your footprints. Slow down enough to notice how your feet and legs move as you walk. Breathe gently, look around and enjoy your surroundings.

If you can't get outdoors, take off your shoes and socks indoors and walk slowly and mindfully around your home. Keep all your attention on your feet. Notice the sensations from different surfaces - carpets, rugs or hard floors. Walk quietly. Be present. Breathe.

Afterwards, sit down or lie down and rest. Notice how you feel now.

DAY FIVE: RESTORATIVE YOGA

When I started going to Restorative Yoga, my husband would ask me what I had done at the class. Like most people he associated Yoga with fancy handstands or learning to tie the body into knots. When I told him, 'Mainly just lying around', it sounded a bit worthless, even to me. I found it difficult to explain why I valued such a minimal-sounding experience.

Restorative Yoga involves a lot of lying down. It can look as if you are doing nothing. And that is actually the point.

We live in a society that prizes action, complexity and achievement. These things are useful, but they have to be balanced by rest and contemplation. Restorative Yoga taught me to take rest seriously. It taught me the power of quiet and slowing down. More than those fancy handstands, rest is a superpower.

Effortless Rest

The main aim of Restorative Yoga is to induce deep, effortless rest. Rest sounds easy, doesn't it? But how easy do you find it to slow down? There is always something else that needs to get done. I tell myself I will sit down after I have cooked this meal or finished this piece of work, but by then another task is demanding my attention. I try to relax, but my mind is racing and I can't get my body comfortable. For me, getting sufficient good quality rest takes real commitment. Rest is a learned skill.

Taking Rest Seriously

Your body needs enough sleep, rest and relaxation. Without all these on a regular basis your health suffers. As well as night time sleep, you also need meaningful and restful breaks during the day. Rest allows your nervous system to find balance and all the systems of your body to function effectively. For the sake of your health, you need to take rest seriously.

Brainwaves

Understanding a little about brainwaves helps explain the importance of rest. The electrical activity of your brain operates at different speeds depending on what you are doing and thinking. This is called brainwave frequency. A frequency is the number of times a wave repeats itself within a second. Frequency is measured in units known as Hertz (Hz). Brainwave frequency can be measured using an electroencephalogram or EEG.

When you are active and alert, your brainwaves will be in the high speed Gamma (over 30Hz) or Beta (13 - 30Hz) patterns. You can process information quickly and make decisions. These states are important for analytical thought. They are also associated with feeling anxious and agitated.

The Alpha state (8 - 12Hz) is one of calm mental resourcefulness. You are relaxed and awake. Yoga, meditation or many of the calm practices in this book will take you into Alpha brainwaves. You feel at ease. This is the perfect state for learning new things.

Theta waves (4-8Hz) arise when you are very relaxed indeed. This is the state of deep meditation. It is the dreamlike space between waking and sleep. You can access Theta brainwaves during Restorative Yoga, Yoga Nidra or a soothing massage. Theta is the perfect state for inner healing and the integration of mind and body.

Delta waves (less than 4Hz) are accessed during deep sleep or states of trance. Some very experienced meditation practitioners can access the Delta state while they are awake, but most of us will be fast asleep.

Restorative Yoga, meditation and other calming practices enable you to slow down your brainwaves at will. Slower brainwaves are associated with enhanced creativity and insight. Often after a deep relaxation or a good night's sleep you can effortlessly solve problems which have been bothering you. Rest really does help you get more done!

Comfortable Supported Yoga Poses

Comfort and support are essential for rest. A wrinkle in a blanket or a slightly misplaced wrist or ankle can be incredibly distracting when you are trying to relax. In Restorative Yoga I use lots of props and supports to help everyone get super comfortable. Bolsters, cushions and folded blankets in exactly the right places make all the difference. You can relax your body and settle into blissful supported rest. Sometimes I also use weighted sandbags and heavy blankets. These help you feel incredibly grounded and calm.

Certain body positions induce states of calm. In Restorative Yoga we move our bodies into different poses, resting in each pose for five to ten minutes or more. The purpose of each position is to relax the body and mind. Poses are designed to access the vagus nerve and the parasympathetic nervous system as well as relieving tension in muscles and fascia. Some of the less obvious positions are the most magical. You might lie on cushions on your belly or extend your legs up against a wall. These poses invoke the restful aspect of the nervous system. You can relax like this for as long as feels good, slowing your brainwaves and enjoying the healing power of rest.

Today's Calm Practice: Reclined Butterfly Pose

Today's calm practice is a Restorative Yoga pose called Reclined Butterfly. Collect together plenty of cushions, plus a blanket or two. A yoga bolster and some yoga blocks or big books are ideal. If you don't have a bolster a really big seat cushion from your settee will do fine. An eye pillow or eye mask will help deepen your relaxation.

Look at the picture below to see me in the reclined butterfly pose. Arrange your big cushions or bolster propped up on some blocks or books to make a gentle slope. Sit down on the floor with the back of your pelvis resting against the end of the bolster or big cushion. Don't sit on the bolster. Slowly lie back so you are lying with your back resting on the bolster and your face looking up towards the ceiling. Check to see if this feels comfortable. You may need to re-arrange the cushions to make sure your lower back and neck are supported and relaxed. You might like another small cushion under your head.

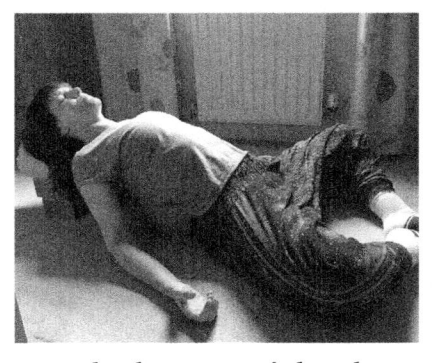

Once your back and neck are happy, bring the soles of your feet together and let your knees drop outwards to the sides. Now place more cushions or blocks under your thighs to support them. If your knees hurt, keep your legs stretched out straight along the floor instead. You might like to try keeping one leg straight and bending the other knee outwards, one leg at a time. If something hurts or feels wrong for you, don't do it. Care for yourself. Nothing should be painful or ache.

You might like to add some cushions or folded blankets under your upper arms. Everything should feel completely supported. You are aiming for total relaxation. Now place an eye pillow over your eyes. Breathe gently and relax.

Stay here for ten minutes or longer. You can follow your breathing with your mind, or allow your thoughts to wander. Listen to some restful music, or enjoy the silence.

When you want to move again, do so slowly and mindfully. Take several minutes to get up very slowly. Enjoy a stretch and maybe a yawn. Notice how you feel after your restorative rest.

DAY SIX: NOURISHING FOOD

I recently blu-tacked a note to the kitchen wall as a reminder for my family. It read, 'If Mum is getting stressed, encourage her to eat some muesli'. I have learned the hard way that low blood sugar makes me feel agitated and angry. In those moments, sitting down and consuming some nourishing carbs will usually avert a furious explosion. Museli works for me because it is quick to prepare and takes a while to eat. Eating, in the right way, helps me stay calm.

Food, stress and calm are intimately related. What I eat and drink affects the way I feel.

Food is an Emotional Issue

Food is an emotional issue. I feel nervous even writing about it. Many people struggle with their weight, body image and guilt about eating habits. Two of my daughters have been seriously unwell with eating disorders. This has made me painfully aware of how bad things can get when a person's relationship with food goes wrong.

When I look at the often bitter debates around the pros and cons of breastfeeding - our first experience with food - I see guilt, anger and fear. We all want feeding our children to be beautiful, natural and easy. How has it become a battlefield?

We are blessed with an abundance of food and choice. Often this choice can overwhelm us. Endless new diet plans vie for our attention, offering to solve all our problems. For people whose relationship with food has got out of control, the most effective solutions are those that offer emotional support and community alongside structure around food itself.

Walking the Tightrope

How can we walk the tightrope between problematic comfort eating and failing to nurture ourselves properly with food? The solution must be holistic. Poor eating habits - whether excessive sugar consumption or skipping meals - do not exist in a vacuum. If we lack calm in the way we nourish our bodies, it is related to a lack of calm in other areas of our lives. For this reason calming practices such as meditation, yoga and gentle holistic therapies can help us eat better. By calming down the nervous system we can diminish our frantic need for the next sugar fix. When I feel kind and loving towards myself I want to nourish my body with good things.

It is one of those virtuous circles. Eating wisely and regularly helps us feel steady and well. Good food regulates our hormones and stabilises our moods. Feeling calm and loving towards ourselves lifts the anxiety around food and helps us eat better. We can improve matters by positively intervening at any point in that circle. Choosing a delicious and healthy meal improves your blood sugar levels and self-esteem. Having a reflexology treatment or taking a walk outdoors relaxes you so that you don't need those sweets to cheer yourself up.

Professional Support

If issues around eating are seriously impacting your health then you should seek professional help and the support of people who love you. Don't struggle alone. Fear and guilt about food may be symptoms of an eating disorder. Obesity threatens your health, but it can be tackled with the right support. Guilt and self-loathing are part of the problem and never the solution. Choosing to love and value yourself is powerful.

Gratitude

Gratitude for our food can help build is healthy and life-affirming. Food is a gift, wonderful and delicious. Whether or not you follow any religious faith, taking a moment to be thankful for your food before eating can help you focus meaningfully on what you are about to eat. Slow down, pause and reflect on the wonderful gift on your plate. Thank everyone who made this meal possible. Nourishment is a joy and a blessing. Eating is one of the precious ways we can enjoy nurturing ourselves, body and mind.

All the Bad Stuff

We all have our weaknesses around food and drink. It helps to know your own particular pitfalls. Try to notice when they are beginning to impact on your wellbeing. Fast-release sugar, caffeine or alcohol can easily become a reward to pick you up when you are feeling down. Before you know it, you have developed an unhelpful habit which can be tricky to break. Instead of beating yourself up about it, try to find a different way to make yourself feel better. Try a short walk outside, spending time with a pet, or sitting down for ten minutes quiet relaxation. You will feel happier and calmer. Perhaps you don't need that chocolate bar right now.

Hydration

Don't forget about hydration too. Drinking enough water, especially in hot weather, can make a huge difference to how you feel. If you have trouble motivating yourself to drink water, try adding low sugar fruit squash or chilling your water in the fridge. Herbal teas can be tasty too.

Dark Chocolate is Good for You

Food is one of the great pleasures of life. It is supposed to make us feel good. I am always encouraged by the many benefits of chocolate. Dark chocolate is rich in iron, antioxidants and flavanols. Eaten in small quantities, it can help protect against cardiovascular disease, Parkinson's and Alzheimer's as well as reducing your risk of inflammatory disorders. It is also delicious!

Today's Calm Practice: Mindful Eating

Nourish your body with something delicious today. Eat mindfully and make it a positive and meaningful experience. Take a little time to choose something you will really enjoy eating, and which will make you feel good. It might be some ripe strawberries, a cooling ice cream or some tasty dark chocolate. Or you could opt for a refreshing drink. It doesn't have to be officially healthy - just something your body and senses will love.

Now sit down somewhere peaceful. Take a few relaxing breaths. Look at your food or drink, and feel thankful. In your mind thank everyone who made this food possible. Thank Nature or God if you believe in him/her. Think about the natural environment your food came from. Imagine it growing in its natural state. Consider the farmers, transport workers and others who have made it available for you today.

Take time to smell, see and appreciate your food or drink. Allow your senses to experience all the colours, shapes and aroma. Then slowly eat or drink, relishing every mouthful. Imagine you are tasting this for the very first time. How does it feel in your mouth and slipping down your throat? How will it nourish and energise your body? Enjoy the enormous pleasure of nourishing yourself.

When you have finished eating, sit quietly for a few minutes.

DAY SEVEN: SECURE AND LOVING TOUCH

Touch is our first sense. At just eight weeks from conception, a human foetus develops the sense of touch, beginning with the face, lips and nose. By twelve weeks the palms of the hands and soles of the feet are sensitive to touch. By seventeen weeks the growing baby can feel touch on its abdomen. Any new mother will tell you that her baby wants to be cuddled and held all the time for comfort. Through our lives, loving and secure touch is calming to our nervous systems. Nature intends us to experience the world through our skin.

Secure and Loving Touch Calms the Nervous System

Secure and loving touch engages the calming parasympathetic nervous system. We all know how soothing a big hug feels when we are agitated or sad. A body massage is wonderfully relaxing. Deep pressure stimulation can be therapeutic for children with autism. It is even helpful for calming patients undergoing wisdom tooth extraction!

Why we Touch our Faces

Since the Covid 19 outbreak we have been advised to try not to touch our faces. However this is really difficult because we instinctively touch our faces to calm ourselves in stressful situations. Touching pressure points on the chin, mouth and forehead causes a relaxing parasympathetic response and makes us feel better. We do it without even realising.

While we all need to practice good hygiene these days, there are plenty of ways we can safely use the power of touch to help ourselves feel calm.

Weighted Blankets

Many people find heavy, weighted blankets helpful for rest, relaxation and sleep. These work on the principle of calming deep pressure stimulation. Gentle pressure on your body calms the nervous system and improves the production of the happy and sleep hormones serotonin and melatonin.

You should choose a blanket that weights about ten per cent or your body weight, or maybe a little more. Never use an adult size weighted blanket for a child. A weighted blanket can be quite expensive but may well be a good investment if you suffer from insomnia or anxiety.

You can achieve some of the same effect by using a heavy quilt or traditional woollen blankets in place of your light and airy duvet. I like to cover my Reflexology clients with a heavy blanket while massaging their feet to enhance the total relaxation experience. Even a normal blanket draped over the body, or a sheet in hot weather, helps us feel settled and secure.

Sandbags

Heavy cotton bags filled with sand or shingle are a one of my favourite props for Restorative Yoga and relaxation. You lie down in a comfortable position, and then position these bags over your legs, back, hips or shoulders. Ideally ask a friend to help you drape and later remove the bags. You can rest like this for as long as you like, feeling incredibly grounded and safe, anchored to the earth. You can purchase sandbags for relaxation from Yoga suppliers, or even make your own.

Eye Pillows

When I was a student midwife, I learned how to resuscitate new babies who need a little help starting to breathe. To do this, you place a mask over the baby's nose and mouth and squeeze in some air to open the lungs and stimulate breathing. You have to be careful not to put pressure on the eye sockets, because pressure around the eyes causes a parasympathetic response. This slows down breathing, which is the exact opposite of what you are trying to achieve. When you keep the mask in the right place, the baby starts breathing quickly and all is well.

Weighted eye pillows work in exactly the opposite way. When you are stressed and agitated you breathe too fast and your heart races. Gentle pressure around the eye sockets causes the parasympathetic response, easing you into the 'rest and digest' state. Your breathing rate and heart rate naturally slow, and you begin to feel calm and relaxed. Relaxing with an eye pillow is a simple and cost-effective way to find calm.

Cuddles, Hugs and Human Connection

Of course loving contact with another human is a brilliant way to find calm. When you get close to people you like your pituitary gland releases the hormone Oxytocin. This happens when you sit and chat with a good friend, when you cuddle your children and when you make love with your partner. Stroking and caressing pets is another good way to release Oxytocin. All these loving connections help you feel happy and calm. Often called 'the love hormone', Oxytocin helps build and sustain nurturing relationships. It is part of why loving touch feels so good.

One of the more hidden costs of the Covid 19 pandemic is the harmful impact of diminished human contact. This is especially difficult for for people who live alone. Everyone needs regular and secure human connection for mental and physical health. When it is safe and comfortable to do so share hugs and kind touch with people close to you (obviously with their consent). Take time to chat and relax with loved ones. Look out for people living on their own and do what you can to connect with them. You will all benefit in so many ways.

Massage

Massage is an intense experience of touch. The giver and receiver of massage both benefit from the close contact and Oxytocin release. There are many types of massage, but essentially massage is an experience of firm and loving touch. Receiving a professional massage from a therapist is wonderfully restful and calming. If you have the time and money, scheduling regular body massage or reflexology (foot massage) into your diary is an excellent way to care for yourself.

You can also massage and be massaged by your family and loved ones. This is easy and lovely to do. You don't need any specialised training or equipment to give a simple massage.

Today's Calm Practice: Calming Massage

If possible, see if you can give or receive a massage today. Alternatively hug someone you love, cuddle a pet, or lie down and relax with an eye pillow.

For massage, don't worry too much about technique. Just make sure both you and the person you are massaging feel safe and comfortable. Stay relaxed, and keep it simple. You can massage someone's back, shoulders or feet by applying gentle pressure with your thumbs, knuckles or the palms of your hands. Either massage over clothes or use oil or cream on bare skin. Be careful not to overdo it and hurt yourself. Avoid massaging on the spine. Let the person you are massaging give you feedback about what they enjoy. Do what feels good for both of you.

If you have children they may enjoy a massage. Or, if you can safely do so, hug or gently massage an elderly relative. Foot massage is great for older people. If you can't get physically close then a socially distanced chat or even a phone call is a precious gift for someone living on their own. You will feel good too.

DAY EIGHT: TURNING UPSIDE DOWN

A ny mention of handstands or headstands at a Yoga class used to make my stomach clench with worry. Like most people I generally feel safest with my feet firmly on the ground. The mere idea of turning upside down (with a balance challenge thrown in) woke up my inner inadequacies.

Yet weirdly when my teacher actually supports me into an upside down pose I feel exhilarated and unexpectedly calm. There are good reasons why the guru B K S Iyengar described headstand and shoulderstand as the king and queen of Yoga poses. Turning yourself upside down has remarkable benefits for both mind and body.

I don't teach handstands or headstands in my Yin and Restorative Yoga classes, but I do include at least one inversion in almost every session. A inversion in Yoga is any position where the head is below the heart. This includes a gentle supported shoulderstand or lying down with your legs up the wall. Downward facing dog and standing forward bend are inversions too. All these poses are good for the circulation, the lymphatic system and the nervous system. They also calm and settle the mind.

Inversions, Blood Pressure and Feeling Calm

Turning yourself upside down has interesting effects on your blood pressure and vagus nerve. This is because your body is brilliant at regulating itself. You have special pressure detectors called baroreceptors in your aortic and carotid arteries in the chest. When you turn upside down, the blood pressure in the area above the heart initially increases due to gravity. More blood is flowing towards the head.

But your clever baroreceptors detect the rise in blood pressure and work rapidly to correct it. They do this by causing a parasympathetic response in the nervous system. This decreases the heart rate and relaxes the blood vessel walls. This has the effect of decreasing blood pressure. It also makes you feel calm.

Turning upside down may initially cause feelings of tension due to both the mental challenge of the position and the rush of blood towards the head. But after a short time the parasympathetic response will bring about a lowering of blood pressure and a sense of stillness and relaxation. With regular practice this stimulation of the baroreceptors improves your ability to regulate your blood pressure.

Health Benefits

B K S Iyengar lists so many benefits for inverted positions. Turning yourself upside down is helpful for insomnia, thyroid function, asthma, constipation, colds, haemorrhoids and hernias. It can alleviate urinary disorders and uterine prolapse. It also helps regulate menstrual flow if done regularly between periods. The mind and body are integrated and calmed. As with all Yoga poses the more often you practice inversions the more your body and mind will benefit.

Legs Up the Wall

Raising your legs above your head in a supported position can be very relaxing. I love the legs up the wall position. Here you can get all the benefits of a gentle inversion without putting pressure on the neck or worrying about balance. Your legs and lower spine work very hard all day supporting your weight. Lying down with your legs up the wall releases this pressure on the lower body. It is especially helpful for varicose veins, swollen ankles and heavy legs. Gravity is your friend, allowing excess fluid to drain out of the legs.

Seeing the World from a Different Angle

When we turn ourselves upside down, we literally see the world from a new angle. Settling and resting into a safe inverted pose can be an opportunity for reflection and meditation. It can help us let go of worries and start afresh.

Staying Safe

You should avoid inverted Yoga poses, especially demanding ones like headstand or full shoulderstand if you have uncontrolled high blood pressure, any problems with your neck or upper spine, headache or migraine. Most yogis recommend avoiding inversions during a menstrual period. If you want to learn headstand or handstand, always seek the help of a qualified Yoga instructor. These poses can be dangerous without proper support and supervision.

Today's Calm Practice: Legs Up the Wall

Relaxing with your legs supported against a wall or door is an easy and accessible way to enjoy the benefits of inversion. Try this today if you are feeling well. Come down out of the pose if it does not feel right for you. Don't try it if you have high blood pressure, migraine, neck problems or you are on your period. Rest lying down in any comfortable position instead.

Find a wall and sit sideways onto the wall with one buttock pressing right up against the base of the wall. Then rotate yourself round so that you are lying on the floor at right angles to the wall, with your legs supported up against the wall. If there is a big gap between your bottom and the base of the wall, come down carefully, move your buttock closer to the wall, and try again.

You can try placing a cushion or folded blanket under your bottom to raise your hips a little higher if you wish.

Make sure you are feeling comfortable here. Check that your lower back and neck feel ok. Avoid turning your neck to one side. Then place an eye pillow over your eyes and relax.

If it feels good, you can stay here for ten to twenty minutes.

Come out of the position slowly and carefully the same way you went in. Lie down on your side for at least five breaths before slowly getting up.

You should feel calm and relaxed. This is a great pose to do before bedtime if you have trouble getting off to sleep.

DAY NINE: CALMING ESSENTIAL OILS

One day I burned my hand with steam from the kettle. It wasn't blistered or serious enough to need medical attention, but I was in quite a bit of pain. Running it under cold water helped, but as soon as the skin dried it hurt again. I started searching the Internet for how to soothe burns. I found several articles about lavender essential oil. Following the instructions, I applied lavender oil to my burn every fifteen minutes or so, until it stopped hurting.

To my amazement, the pain was completely gone within less than an hour. The skin healed quickly with no redness. Nowadays I always keep a bottle of lavender essential oil in my kitchen drawer to treat minor burns.

You should always begin by cooling a burn under cold running water for as long as possible. Always seek medical attention for serious burns or scalds and for young children.

Powerful Properties

Calming essential oils are powerful. The remarkable properties of lavender, frankincense and many other distilled plant oils can hugely impact your mood and well-being.

Lavender is one of my favourite essential oils. It is safe, gentle and has wonderful calming and healing properties. The essential oil is steam distilled from freshly cut flowers. I love the clean, refreshing aroma which instantly soothes.

Lavender essential oil has sedative, anti-spasmodic, local anaesthetic, stress reducing and anti-microbial properties. For most people it is safe to use directly on the skin (unlike most essential oils) as it is non-irritating. Lavender is known as 'the mother oil' because it is good for virtually everything. It is helpful for skin healing, immunity, headaches, period pains, anxiety, depression, insomnia and more. If you are feeling upset, lavender can make you feel better.

Cleansing and Calming a Room

I love the way lavender cleanses a space, physically and energetically. A couple of drops of lavender oil in a diffuser calms the atmosphere in a room, influencing everyone present. You might like to try diffusing lavender in your home and notice the subtle effects. Tensions will be reduced and everyone will feel more settled and relaxed. You can also mix a few drops of lavender oil with water in a spray bottle, shake it up, and use it as a natural deodorising room spray. This is much healthier than commercial chemical air-fresheners. The antiseptic properties of lavender help to create a clean and healthy space. Lavender brings calm.

Promoting Restful Sleep

Lavender's sleep-inducing properties are well known. Lavender oil contains Linalyl acetate and Linalool which are natural sedatives. A couple of drops of lavender oil on a tissue on your pillow helps you settle down for a good night's sleep. Use eye pillows containing dried lavender flowers to enhance and deepen relaxation. You can also use lavender in your bath, adding 8 - 12 drops of essential oil to some full fat milk or unscented bubble bath before dispersing it into warm water. Avoid adding undiluted oils to a bath. They will not disperse well and might irritate your skin.

Natural Painkiller

Lavender's anti-spasmodic and anti-inflammatory effects make it a brilliant natural painkiller. For a headache add a couple of drops of lavender oil to a cloth wrung out in cool water. Then use this as a cold compress over your forehead. To make a massage oil you can add 6 drops of essential oil to two tablespoons of a safe base oil such as organic sunflower or grapeseed oil. Massage the oil into the skin. It will ease aches and pains. Enjoy the feeling of soothing calm.

Perfumes and Memories

Not everyone likes lavender. Scents are processed in the same region of your brain as memories and emotions. This is why an aroma can instantly take you back to a specific place or person. If you had an unpleasant relative or mean teacher who liked to use lavender perfumed soap, you may hate the smell of lavender. You might not even remember the reason but lavender evokes strong negative emotions in some people.

Frankincense

If you are not a fan of lavender, or if you would just like to try something different, frankincense is another wonderful calming essential oil. Frankincense is distilled from the resin of an African tree. Its essential oil is brilliant for emotional healing, digestion, stress management, inflammation and pain reduction. Like lavender, frankincense helps to heal damaged skin. It makes excellent anti-aging creams and serums.

Blissful Biochemicals

Frankincense increases the production of calming biochemicals in the body. When you inhale frankincense or massage it into the skin you make more soothing endorphins. You also produce a substance called phenylethylamine (PEA) which works in the limbic area of the brain to create a feeling of bliss. Frankincense helps reduce the cortisol stress response and calms down chronic stress. It is an excellent oil to use for anxiety, fear and panic attacks.

Frankincense essential oil can be used in the same ways as lavender. You can use it in a diffuser or a room spray, on a compress or in a bath. Never take any essential oils internally in food or drink, and avoid using undiluted oils neat on the skin. Use small amounts - just a few drops at a time is plenty. Remember that these are strong, concentrated distillations. Less is more.

Other Oils to Try

Some other calming essential oils include rose, geranium and chamomile oils. These calming oils all blend well with citrus oils such as mandarin or bergamot for a cheering and uplifting effect.

Purchasing Essential Oils

Always buy essential oils from a reputable supplier. They should come in dark glass bottles, labelled with the Latin botanical name. Beware very cheap products, and anything labeled 'fragrance'. These may be imitations based on petrochemicals which can be harmful to your health.

Today's Calm Practice: Aromatherapy Shower

I love using essential oils in the shower. Try putting two drops of lavender or frankincense essential oil on a facecloth and using this to sponge yourself down in a long relaxing shower. Alternatively you can use calming essential oils in any of the ways described above.

You will feel cleansed, calm and refreshed.

DAY TEN: COOL WATER

Last year I went to a Wim Hof method workshop. Wim is a remarkable Dutchman who has pioneered ways to become 'happy, strong and healthy' using breathing exercises and cold water immersion. Part of the workshop involved immersion in a tub of ice water. This was done outdoors in December. To my amazement I found the experience both exhilarating and calming.

Cool water and calm are best friends. Water makes up about sixty percent of our bodies. We count aquatic mammals like seals and whales among our evolutionary ancestors. Renewing that basic relationship with water can help us find calm.

The Autonomic Nervous System

Now I know what you are thinking. The very idea of being immersed in icy water is awful. It's difficult to imagine anything less calming. And yes, immersion in cold water does cause a big initial 'fight or flight' response. If you have ever been swimming outdoors in a cool lake or ocean, you will recall that gasp and the feeling of your heart racing when your shoulders dip under the water. The nervous system responds automatically to the challenge of this chilly environment by increasing your heart rate and putting you on full alert. You may feel excited and exhilarated.

If you stay in the water another effect soon emerges. You begin to feel calmer. This is partly because you are relaxing into this new environment and partly due to the dive reflex.

The Dive Reflex

The dive reflex goes right back to your aquatic mammalian ancestors. Humans have a built-in response to immersion in cool water. It works best when the face and nostrils get wet and when you hold your breath underwater. Your body knows it needs to preserve oxygen underwater so the dive reflex takes over. Your heart rate slows down and the calming parasympathetic side of the nervous system is activated. Your blood is redirected to your important internal organs to keep you alive underwater.

Anxiety and Panic Attacks

Splashing your face with cool water or even immersing your face in a bowl of water is an effective way to cope with panic attacks and anxiety. This is due to the dive reflex. Water around the nostrils and holding your breath underwater naturally slows down your heart rate and breathing. This can be very helpful if you are feeling anxious and you are struggling to control your emotions. You will quickly feel calmer and more able to cope.

Heart Rate Variability and Long Term Stress

If you have long term stress, maybe due to a tough job or a difficult family situation, you can sometimes get stuck in a state of constant anxiety. Your ability healthily to handle stress is damaged. You find it difficult to move from excitement to calm and back again.

For long term health and wellbeing you need balance between the two sides of the nervous system. This can be measured as heart rate variability. The amount of time between each heartbeat should not always be exactly the same. Having some variation in the time between beats is a healthy sign that your autonomic nervous system can switch readily between the sympathetic and parasympathetic modes. Low heart rate variability has been associated with an increased risk of heart attacks and strokes.

When I worked as a midwife we kept a close eye on the heart rate variability of babies during more complex births. If the heart rate variability was low it meant the baby was becoming too stressed by the birth process and might need some help to be born safely.

Raising Your Heart Rate and Slowing it Down Again

All this means that activities that first raise your heart rate and then slow it down again are good for you. They help your nervous system get used to switching between the excited and calm states. Cold water immersion does this particularly well. Any type of challenging exercise followed by relaxation is good too. This is one of the reasons why lying down for relaxation at the end of a Yoga class is so important.

Cool Showers

Taking a cooler shower than usual is a safe and accessible way to explore cool water and calm. Since the Wim Hof workshop I now regularly turn down the temperature at the end of my shower. It makes me feel good at the start of my day.

You can wash yourself at your normal warm shower temperature and then turn the dial down at the end. You can turn it down a little bit or a lot. It's up to you. The cold water will make you gasp at first but then you can let yourself relax into it. Splashing it on your face will help you calm down. Afterwards you feel fantastic. Why not give it a try?

Outdoor Swimming, Paddling and Playfulness

I am a big fan of outdoor swimming. Being around lakes and the sea brings us closer to nature and helps us feel good. Paddling in shallow waves is a great way to release your inner child and have fun. Being around natural water is relaxing.

Stay Safe

Of course water can be dangerous. Don't try cold water immersion if you have any heart problems. Never swim alone. If you want to try open water swimming the safest way is to join a group or find a qualified instructor. Be very careful about any outdoor body of water. The excellent Outdoor Swimming Society has lots of great information about safety on their website. Please have a read if you are thinking about swimming outside.

Today's Calm Practice: Take a Cool Shower

Today try turning down the temperature of your shower after you have finished washing. Expect to gasp a little. Tell yourself this is lovely and refreshing. Stay calm - it's only cold water! Allow yourself to breathe. Experience the cool water on your skin. See if you can count slowly to ten. Enjoy the sensations. Take time to notice how you feel afterwards.

If you have the opportunity you might like to take a paddle or a little dip in some water outdoors. Be sure to stay safe. Have fun.

BREATH

DAY ELEVEN: BREATH AWARENESS

When I have trouble getting off to sleep I count my breaths. Nine times out of ten (the tenth is usually when I have massively overdosed on caffeine) this sends me off to the land of dreams long before I reach one hundred. It is simple and effective. Breath awareness works.

Breath awareness is a superpower. Humans have an exceptionally subtle ability to control and think about our own breathing. This goes alongside our highly developed speech skills. By focusing on our breath, we can directly control our nervous system, body and mind.

One of the Most Ancient Forms of Meditation

Breath awareness is one of the most ancient forms of meditation. People have been practising meditation for much longer than they have been writing about it. Meditating on the breath is referred to in scriptures from Buddhist, Vedic, Sufi, Jainist and other traditions. Nowadays many people use breath awareness as part of Mindfulness practice. It is widely prescribed as therapy for anxiety, chronic pain and other health conditions.

Your Breath is Always Here

Your breath is accessible. It is always here. You don't have to go looking for your meditation beads or find a book. You are always breathing, so you can choose to focus on it any time and anywhere. When I used to commute to work I often closed my eyes on the train and rested my mind on my breath for a few minutes. It is a reliable way to feel better.

Unlocking Control of the Nervous System

You breathe all the time without thinking about it. Your brainstem keeps you breathing so you can stay alive even when you are asleep. But you can choose to notice your breath whenever you wish. You can access feelings of calm by deliberately changing the way you breathe.

If something gives you a fright - a door slamming,

perhaps, or a firework exploding - your heart rate and breathing speeds up up all by itself. This prepares you to take quick action to deal with danger. But once you realise there is nothing to worry about you take some long, deep breaths to calm yourself down. Gradually your heart stops racing and that horrible shaky feeling subsides. Those slow breaths have calmed your nervous system. Your breathing helps control how you feel.

How to Meditate on the Breath

There are lots of ways to meditate on the breath. Different people prefer different approaches so it is worth experimenting to see what works for you. You may find your preferences change as you become more experienced.

Counting Breaths

I used to find breath counting really boring. It is worth persevering through the boredom because this is a powerful practice. In a way boredom is part of the experience because meditation aims to settle down a busy mind.

Your over-stimulated mind is a bit like a fun-loving monkey, leaping and jumping all over the place. Sometimes the monkey needs to calm down and have a rest. Counting your breaths gives the monkey mind something to do. To begin with it resists. It wants to play and swing from the trees. You feel bored and frustrated. But if you keep gently reminding the monkey to sit quietly and count it will gradually relax and slow down. You begin to feel much better.

How to Count Your Breaths

Here's how to do a simple breath counting meditation. Sit or lie down comfortably and close your eyes. Take a few minutes simply to become aware of your breathing. When you are ready, begin to count your breaths. You can count 'one' on the in-breath and 'two' on the out-breath and so on. Alternatively you can count an entire in-breath and out-breath as 'one', and the next complete breath as 'two'. Just be consistent and keep counting until you get to 'ten'. Then begin again at 'one'.

Coming back to 'one' after each count of ten is a good way to make sure you are still focusing on the breath. It is very easy to just keep on counting on and on automatically without realising what you are doing. Trust me - I've done this plenty of times!

Losing Count

Almost certainly you will lose count. Either you will get to 'thirty-eight' with absolutely no idea how you arrived here, or you will find yourself thinking about what to cook for dinner tonight, or Auntie Jean's birthday next Tuesday. This is completely normal. Don't feel bad about it. Just begin again at 'one' and then 'two' and so on.

Feeling the Breath

Another approach is to focus on what it feels like to breathe. Become very curious about your breath. Try to notice everything about it. Where do you feel the breath most easily? Is it in your chest, your throat or at your nostrils? How warm is the air at the nostrils? Is it warmer when you breathe out? Does it tickle a little? Does your breath feel tighter or easier today? Can you feel your breastbone or your ribs moving? Can your hear the sound of your own breath?

When your mind wanders off on its monkey meanderings to another subject bring it back gently to the experience of breathing. Don't get annoyed with yourself. Your brain is made for thinking about lots of stuff. Focusing on one thing like the breath is a skill learned by practice.

Simple Breath Awareness

Some people can stay aware of their breath without needing to count or consciously experience sensations. This can be quite difficult. For most people a practice like counting helps them stay focused, at least to begin with. But you may enjoy just noticing your breath coming in and going out like waves on the seashore. Try it and see.

Don't Try to Change Anything

Breath awareness is simply being aware of the breath as it is. You don't need to change anything. Over the next few days we will look calming practices which involve deliberately changing your breath patterns. But there is huge value in simply paying attention to your natural breath.

So don't worry about how fast or slow, easy or tight your breathing seems to be. Accept it however it is. Most likely your breathing will slow down as you relax into the meditation, but your focus is simply to stay aware of the breath. This awareness will calm your mind and body all by itself.

Be Kind to Yourself

Most people find breath awareness difficult to begin

with. And it often continues to be challenging even after quite a bit of practice. So when your mind wanders away from the breath for the twentieth time, be kind to yourself. Don't feel bad or beat yourself up. It is normal and natural for the mind to want to be busy. You are training it to slow down and rest. This is a journey of discovery. It takes time.

Today's Calm Practice: Breath Counting Meditation

Sit or lie comfortably for five to ten minutes. Allow your mind to take a rest by focusing on your breath. Make this a nice little break in your day. I strongly recommend the breath counting approach for beginners. Set a timer when you begin so you won't have to worry about when to finish. Notice how you feel afterwards.

DAY TWELVE: BELLY BREATHING

Have you ever watched a baby breathing? If so, you will noticed her belly gently rising and falling with each breath. Babies naturally breathe using the diaphragm muscle. But as we get older we often breathe shallowly into the upper part of our lungs, over-using our upper chest and neck muscles. This can contribute to stress, anxiety and many health problems. Breathing as you breathed as a baby can help you relax and feel calm.

Belly breathing is calming, relaxing and good for your health. Today we will focus on probably the simplest and most natural of breathing exercises: breathing deep into your belly.

What is the Diaphragm?

Your diaphragm is a big dome-shaped sheet of muscle attached to your spine and lower ribs. It is shaped is a bit like a parachute. It divides your chest from your abdomen. It is your primary breathing muscle. The diaphragm is also involved in changing the pressure in your abdomen when you wee, poo and vomit. It helps prevent acid reflux too.

The diaphragm moves down when you breathe in. This expands the space in your chest and creates a vacuum to bring air into the lungs. The diaphragm moves up again when you breathe out, relaxing back to its resting position and helping push the air out.

Diaphragmatic Breathing and Belly Breathing

The terms 'diaphragmatic breathing' and 'belly breathing' are often used interchangeably. You use your diaphragm to breathe all the time. But by deliberately focusing on breathing 'into the belly' you can use the diaphragm more than usual. Your lungs don't really go down into your belly, but when you breathe deeply into the bottom of the lungs the diaphragm presses down on the abdominal organs. This makes your belly swell a little as your breathe in. Then when you exhale, the belly relaxes and flattens as the diaphragm rises. Breathing deeply in this way exercises the diaphragm, massages the abdominal organs and helps you feel calm.

The Vagus Nerve

Remember the vagus nerve? It's a key component of your parasympathetic nervous system, which gets you into a calm and restful state. The vagus nerve passes right through your diaphragm. When you breathe deeply into your belly, the vagus nerve helps your body slow down and relax. Research shows that regular belly breathing can reduce inflammation in the body. This can decrease your risk of lots of serious health conditions like inflammatory bowel disease, heart disease, cancer, stroke, diabetes and sepsis. It also greatly improves the strength of your immune system.

Belly breathing is one of the simplest breath exercises you can do. It is often practised at Yoga classes, but you can easily do it at home too.

Today's Calm Practice: Belly Breathing

You might like to set a timer on your phone for, say, ten minutes before you begin.

You need to lie down for this one. Get yourself comfortable lying on a firm surface. Lie on your back. A yoga mat or rug on the floor is ideal.

Make sure you are comfortable and warm. A cosy blanket and snuggly socks might be nice.

You can put a small cushion under your head if you like. Make sure your neck is comfortable.

You might also like to put a bolster, cushion or support under your knees. This can help your lower back relax.

Close your eyes and place both hands gently on your belly.

Breathe in and out through your nose if possible.

Gradually deepen your breaths so that you can feel your belly rise under your hands as you breathe in. Imagine your breath going right down into your belly.

Notice how your belly softens and sinks back down again as you breathe out.

Focus on sending each breath deep down into the belly.

If you like you can count as you breathe in and out. For example you might like to count 1-2-3-4 as you breathe in and then 1-2-3-4 again as you breathe out. This can help you stay focused.

If you feel you want to pause between breathing in and breathing out, do so. Let any pause between the breaths arise naturally. Don't force it.

You may well find your breathing naturally slows down as you breathe into your belly. Just allow this to happen. Don't force anything.

Keep breathing into your belly for five to ten minutes. Then let your breathing return to a natural breath and relax.

Rest for another minute or two before getting up. Notice how you feel now.

Enjoy the rest of your day.

Belly breathing is great to do before bedtime as it helps you relax ready for a good night's sleep.

DAY THIRTEEN: ALTERNATE NOSTRIL BREATHING

Students often arrive at a Yoga class bringing all sorts of worries and agitation from their daily lives. Sometimes I turn up to teach a class feeling stressed and out of sorts. Alternate nostril breathing is a reliable way of settling myself and everyone else down. It is one of my go-to practices for calm.

An Ancient Yogic Practice

Alternate nostril breathing is a calming and balancing practice. It has been taught as part of Yoga for many centuries. In Sanskrit alternate nostril breathing is known as *Shodhana Nadi Pranayama.* This means channel clearing breath practice. Yoga philosophy teaches that we have lots of energy channels in our bodies, known as nadis. Blockages in these channels can result in all sorts of health problems.

Two of the main nadis are called Pingala and Ida. These are believed to spiral around the spinal column in a double helix shape. They correspond to the two sides of the personality - hot and cold, sun and moon, active and passive. Part of the goal of Yoga practice is to balance these two aspects of the person.

Brain Hemispheres and Balance

This ancient belief system has many parallels in modern science. The two main nadis relate closely to the two hemispheres of the brain. The left side of the brain deals primarily with cool, logical thought, while the right brain hemisphere is responsible for creativity, passion and emotion. This is remarkably similar to the Yogic Ida and Pingala division. Most of us have natural tendencies to be led by either head or heart. But we can all recognise the benefits of balance.

Breathing through One Nostril at a Time

Everyone naturally tend to breathe mostly through one nostril at a time. You have a nasal cycle which is controlled by your autonomic brain function. Without you consciously realising it your brain directs more blood flow to one nostril, causing that nostril to open up more and let more air through. After a while it switches over to the other nostril. The timing of the cycle varies between individuals. It can be as short as twenty-five minutes or as long as eight hours. In most people it is around every one and a half to two hours.

There are several reasons your body does this. The nostril cycle is thought to be related to making sure one nostril is always moist. This keeps your sense of smell healthy. The nostril cycle also encourages you to turn over in bed regularly at night to avoid bedsores. There is scientific evidence that a number of serious diseases are correlated with problems with nasal cycle. It seems that those ancient Yogis knew what they were talking about!

A Calming Effect

The practice of deliberately breathing through alternate nostrils helps re-set and re-balance the natural nasal cycle. It lowers the heart rate and reduces stress and anxiety. The quiet and concentration required to do the practice also has a relaxing and calming effect.

Today's Calm Practice: Alternate Nostril Breathing

Find a quiet space where you will not be disturbed.

Sit in a comfortable upright position. You can sit in a chair with your feet flat on the floor or sit on a cushion on the floor. Sit cross-legged only if you can do so comfortably for five to ten minutes.

Make sure your spine is upright and relaxed.

You might like a cushion to support your elbow.

Get Ready

Allow your left hand to rest in your lap. (If you are left handed, you may swap hands if you prefer.). With your right hand, fold down your index and middle fingers towards the palm. You should have the thumb and fourth fingers sticking up on your right hand. Refer to the picture below to see the correct hand position.

Breathe in and out through your nose for a few breaths. Become aware of your breath.

Breathe through Alternate Nostrils

When you feel ready gently close your right nostril with your right thumb. Inhale through your left nostril. Then close your left nostril with your fourth finger. Open the right nostril and breathe out slowly.

Keep the right nostril open and breathe in through the right nostril. Then close it with your thumb and breathe out through the left nostril. This is one complete cycle.

Continue breathing like this for maybe ten to twenty breath cycles, or longer if you wish. Keep your posture upright and your shoulders relaxed.

You may notice your breathing slowing down as you relax into the pattern. You may also like to pause between the breaths if that feels good.

Let Your Breath Return to Normal

When you feel ready, let your hand relax to your lap and allow your breathing to return to its natural pattern. Sit quietly for a while and enjoy the feeling of calm and relaxation.

Have a go at alternate nostril breathing today. It will help you feel calm and benefit your health and wellbeing all day long. Some people like to do this as a regular practice at the start of each day.

DAY FOURTEEN: OCEAN BREATH

I love the sound of waves on a beach. The gentle breath of the sea is constant, rising and falling in an eternal rhythm. It makes me feel quiet and secure.

I think part of the reason we find wave sounds so calming is because they correspond to the natural inhalation and exhalation of our breathing. The sea echoes the flow of our life.

Ujjayi Breath

Ujjayi breath is a breathing practice often used in Yoga. The Sanskrit name means 'Victorious breath'. It is so called because the practice builds positive control over both body and mind, leading to inner calm. This way of breathing is also known as 'Ocean breath' because it sounds like the sea.

Benefits of Controlling the Breath

Ocean breath or Ujjayi breath involves a slight restriction at the back of the throat, together with steady inhalations and exhalations. You breathe through the nose, keeping the mouth softly closed. Your breath is relaxed and controlled.

The effects are very calming and steadying. Ocean breath is coupled with sequences of poses in Ashtanga or Vinyasa Yoga classes to create focused and mindful movement. But it is also a hugely beneficial practice on its own or with meditation.

Ocean breathing slows down the breath. It encourages you to focus your mind on your breathing. When you slow your breath your heartbeat slows down too. The body settles into the calm 'rest and digest' state.

The Parasympathetic State

The vagus nerve is the key to unlocking your calm parasympathetic nervous system. This important nerve passes through the neck. It is affected by the throat constriction and steady breath pattern when you practice Ocean breathing. That means Ocean breath is a reliable way to manage anxiety and panic attacks. You will quickly feel relaxed and calm.

Like all practices that help us enter the parasympathetic state, Ocean breathing is good for long term health. By settling the mind and relaxing the body it helps prevent and manage conditions related to inflammation and stress. These include bowel conditions, cancers, heart disease, depression, diabetes and high blood pressure.

Focus and Concentration

Regular breath practices are great for focus and concentration. You are learning to settle your busy mind. If you are easily distracted or forgetful Ocean breathing can you focus. When you have an important task to complete you can work more efficiently and get more done.

Meditation and Visualisation

Ocean breathing works well with meditation and visualisation. You can enter a meditative state by simply focusing on your breath. I like to visualise waves on the seashore as I breathe. If you are lucky enough to be able to visit a beach you can try watching the waves and breathing with them.

How to do Ocean Breathing

You need to sit upright for this one. Sit on a cushion on the floor or on an upright chair. Make sure you are comfortable and your hips are higher than your knees. If you are on a chair your feet should be resting flat on the floor.

Relax your shoulders and grow tall through your

spine. Make sure your core muscles are supporting your lower back.

Now drop your chin slightly downwards towards your chest.

Try breathing through out through your mouth first

Imagine you are breathing on a mirror and you want to make mist on it with your breath. Breathe out gently through your mouth making a soft 'haaaaaa' sound. Visualise the mirror steaming up. Do this a few times. Notice how this breath feels in your throat.

Now breathe through your nose

Now close your mouth and breath in and out through your nose. Try to make the same soft 'haaaaa' sound at the back of your throat. Some people say this sounds a bit like Darth Vader! I prefer to think about waves on the shore or the sound a seashell makes when you hold it up to your ear.

The sound and the feeling should be soft and gentle like a whisper. It should not be uncomfortable in your throat but there should be a slight feeling of constriction.

Keep Breathing Regularly

Keep breathing in and out like this. Use your nose to breathe and make that gentle whispering sound inside your throat. Imagine the waves on the sea on a lovely sunny day as you inhale and exhale.

To help yourself breathe steadily you might like to count in your head. You can count 1-2-3-4 as you breathe in and then 1-2-3-4 as you breathe out. Don't try to hold your breath or breathe in or out for longer than is comfortable. You are aiming for an easy, steady rhythm.

Today's Calm Practice: Ocean Breathing

Today find somewhere quiet to sit and try Ocean breathing. Visualise the gentle waves lapping on the shore. Breathe calmly and relax.

DAY FIFTEEN: CHANTING AND SINGING

Humans have been singing or chanting together for millenia. Whether at a place of worship, a sports stadium, a yoga studio or a party, uniting our voices unites us as a community. In shared song we bring our breath, our emotions and our values together as one. The simple fun of singing 'Happy Birthday' joins family and friends in celebration. Singing and building community belong together.

The loss of shared singing and chanting is one of the tragedies of the Covid 19 pandemic. I very much hope that we will not be without this key human activity for too long. It is important for our wellbeing.

Singing and Breathing

When you sing or chant you naturally regulate your breathing. I have talked about belly breath and ocean breath as helpful practices for calm and health. Singing gives us the benefits of both these practices without having to think about it.

When you chant or sing with enthusiasm you open up your lungs and breathe deeply. All good singing teachers tell their students to stand or at least sit upright to sing. This opens the chest and allows the diaphragm to move freely. When you sing you breathe from the diaphragm and exchange plenty of oxygen and carbon dioxide through your lungs. You practice good posture. You also engage the calming aspects of your nervous system by activating the vagus nerve. Naturally you feel better.

Singing requires control of the breath passing through the vocal cords. This has similarities with the ocean breath or ujjayi breath where you breathe with control in the throat. Some singers recommend ujjayi breath to improve breath control. Singing is all about the breath. And the breath is a gateway to calm and better health.

Singing Releases Tension

When you sing your brain releases endorphins and oxytocin. These natural neurotransmitters and hormones help you feel positive, calm and connected. Making tuneful sounds releases tension. There is plenty of evidence that singing relieves depression, lowers levels of the stress hormone cortisol and boosts feelings of confidence.

Singing and Mindfulness

When you chant or sing you focus completely on the experience. The combination of the sounds, the words and the breathing makes it easy to be present in the moment. This is one of the reasons chanting and meditation or prayer are so closely connected in many traditions. Chanting words to music helps centre the mind and brings you readily into a calm and meditative state. You can let go of your worries and feel part of something larger than yourself.

Singing for Rhythm and Confidence

I sometimes sing while I swim, especially when I am struggling with my breathing or confidence. Singing reminds me to breathe out regularly. It also helps me get into a steady rhythm with my stroke. This gets rid of panicky feelings and lets me enjoy the experience.

Plenty of us sing in the shower. This is a private and watery place where we feel free to be ourselves. A nice loud song creates a mood of confidence and wellbeing at the start of the day. Your family might even enjoy it too!

Many speakers and performers practice voice exercises before going on stage (or on Zoom nowadays!). This is as important for calming nerves as it is for waking up the voice.

Yoga and Kirtan

I love song and chant in many traditions. Gentle Taize chants, stirring hymns and loud Abba renditions at parties all have the power to move me. In the Yoga world we have Kirtan, which is the chanting of Sanskrit mantras. This is a very beautiful experience.

Kirtan originates in the Indian Bhakti tradition which focuses on devotion and love for the Divine. Many of the mantras used in Kirtan refer to Hindu deities. Some people from different faith backgrounds might be uncomfortable with this, and I would never advise you to sing something which does not feel right for you. The benefits of song come from our sense of union with the whole experience. Personally I like to think of the ancient sacred sounds of Kirtan as symbols and representatives of universal truths.

Chanting Om

I usually close my Yoga classes with a shared chant of Om. Om or Aum is said to be the primordial sound of the Universe. The earth as it turns makes deep sounds, far too low for human hearing. Maybe this is the Om. This sound is believed to connect us to ourselves, one another and to universal energies. Certainly it has the power to calm and unite.

Feeling Nervous about Singing

People often feel nervous or shy about singing or chanting in public. Maybe you were once told by a teacher that you were out of tune. Or perhaps you worry about what your voice will sound like. I encourage you to let go of your fears and simply sing out, maybe in private or in the shower to begin with. Sing aloud and you will feel good.

Hopes for the Future

I feel sad that, for now, I cannot share a deep Om with Yogis in my studio. I grieve that I cannot join in a Kirtan group or sing hymns at church. I hope and pray that this time of pandemic will quickly pass and we will soon be able to sing and chant together again. I believe it is crucial for sustaining human communities.

For now we can enjoy singing alone or in our family groups. Let's make the most of it!

Today's Calming Practice: Singing or Chanting

Today I encourage you to do some singing or chanting, either alone or with your family. When the pandemic is over and it is safe to do so you might like to sing with friends or a community group.

Here are some suggestions:

Sing your favourite song in the shower

Go for a walk and sing as you walk. Maybe put on headphones and sing along. Ignore any funny looks from passers-by!

Chant Om ten times. More if you like!

Find a Kirtan session online and join in.

Notice how you feel afterwards.

NATURE

DAY SIXTEEN: WALKING OUTDOORS

Walking has been my lifeline during the Covid 19 lockdowns. In times of fear and tension I escape into nature and rest in the rhythm of my footsteps. I have discovered new and lovely places to walk near my home. A path beside a stream leads me to a quiet wood. Under a tunnel of trees I watch cows snoozing beside a pond. I watch the seasons change and the skies expand. My daily walks soothe me and help me cope with uncertainty and disappointment.

Walking Outdoors is Good for You

Walking outdoors can lower blood pressure, reduce stress hormones, improve immunity and calm your nervous system. Regularly exercising your legs is crucial for the health of your brain and nervous system. It is even better if you can walk in a park or the countryside. Our early human ancestors spent most of their lives outdoors. There is increasing evidence that urban environments overstimulate the prefrontal cortex of the brain, leading to a myriad of health problems. Spending time in green spaces makes you feel better.

Walking in New and Familiar Places

I love discovering new places on foot. Walking is a slow and gentle way to explore a space. I wonder what views or pleasant surprises might be around the next corner. When I arrive somewhere on holiday I don't feel settled until I have taken a walk around my new environment. A simple stroll grounds me. I begin to feel safe and at home.

But there is something special about walking familiar routes too. Close to home you don't have to worry about getting lost. You have time to enjoy the subtle changes in the weather and seasons. You notice a new bird in the hedgerow. Rabbits in the fields. Day by day ferns unfurl and flowers grow tall. You see brambles flower and blackberries change colour. Fluffy seedheads attract finches. Birdsong subtly changes and mushrooms sprout as autumn ripens. Fresh rain fills puddles which reflect the sky. Your local walk is a daily journey of discovery.

Walking in All Weathers

We all enjoy walking on a sunny day. But sometimes it can be exhilarating to walk in other weathers too. One evening my home was busy and noisy and I needed to escape for a while. Torrential rain was splashing off the roads, but I put on a coat and went out anyway. I strode out through the storm, hearing thunder clash and watching the lightning. I came home drenched but refreshed, feeling much calmer for my encounter with the rawness of nature. A little wildness can soothe the soul.

Silence, Music and Stories

I often try to leave my phone at home when I walk. That way I can lose myself in the experience of being outdoors. Freed from distractions, I let my thoughts drift and enjoy the unfolding world around me.

But other times I like to listen to music or maybe an audiobook. If it is difficult to motivate myself to get outdoors, the opportunity to hear the next chapter of an exciting story can make all the difference. Listening to a favourite song can help my steps skip along. Sometimes I join in and sing too - usually when I think no one is listening!

Meditation, Prayer and Pilgrimage

Walking is a wonderful opportunity for meditation and prayer. The rhythm of your footsteps helps your thoughts flow freely. Even in an urban environment you can see the sky and other reminders of realities greater than yourself. It is easy to settle the mind and focus the heart. Your life appears in a bigger context. It is easier to become aware of things you might like to change or people who need your loving attention.

Many faith traditions share the concept of pilgrimage - a special journey to a sacred place. Pandemic has made many physical pilgrimages impossible for the time being. But you can still assign meaning and purpose to your walking. You could even dedicate it to a person or cause close to your heart.

In the summer of 2020 I completed a virtual Camino de Santiago. I walked the 480 miles of this traditional Spanish pilgrimage along the pavements, fields and sea wall paths of Essex, my home county. It was a beautiful and enriching experience. One day I hope to follow the route through Northern Spain. You might like to think of ways you can assign meaning to your daily walks, even close to home.

Walking Where You Are - City, Sea and Forest

We all have different environments available to us. If you live in a city perhaps you can walk in a park or beside a river or canal. Getting outside and feeling the air on your face and seeing the sky will calm and settle you. Even walking around streets and beside buildings can be relaxing.

I particularly enjoy walking beside the sea. The salt air blowing across the marshes seems to cleanse my mind. Walking on a beach is extra good exercise too as you march across sand and shingle.

Many people report huge benefits to their mood and sense of wellbeing from spending time in forests. Forest Bathing, known in Japanese as *Shinrin Yoku*, is a growing movement in the UK. Immersing yourself in the sights, aromas and peace of a woodland or forest can help you relax, enhancing your health and wellbeing.

Today's Calm Practice: Walking Outdoors

Go for a walk outdoors today. If it is cold or raining, wrap up warm and wear a good waterproof coat and boots. Go somewhere with green space, trees or water is possible. Leave your phone at home. The world can survive without you for a little while. Breathe deeply. Pay attention to the sights and sounds of nature. Let your senses enjoy the experience. Come home feeling calm.

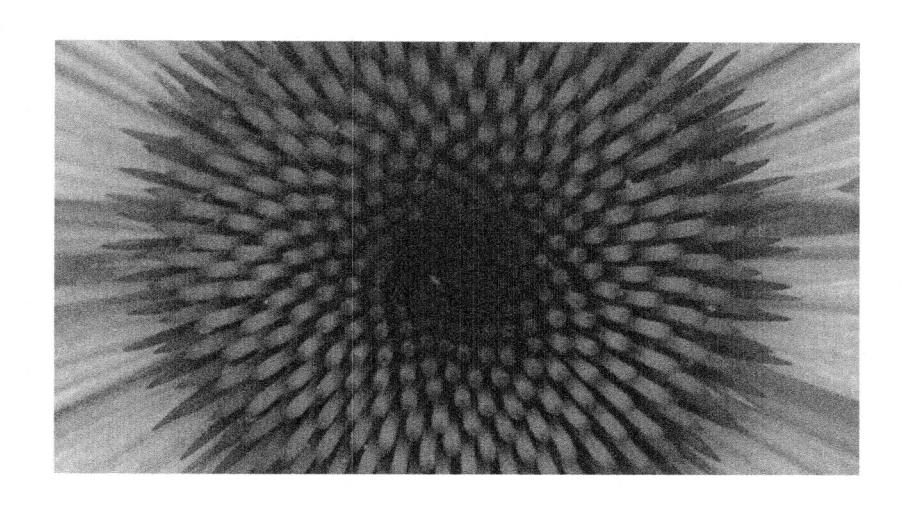

DAY SEVENTEEN: NATURE MEDITATION

In spring and summer I often sit in a quiet corner of my garden to reflect and meditate. Here I have planted lavenders and brightly coloured flowers which attract bees, especially on sunny days. Few things are more peaceful than watching a bee visiting one flower after another, intent on its purpose. I love looking at its soft furry body and listening to its gentle hum. Sitting here surrounded by nature I feel soothed and settled.

Retreating into Nature

It is no accident that many retreat centres and monasteries are found in remote and beautiful locations. Humans have known for thousands of years that it is easier to calm our minds when we escape the crowds and get close to nature. Deserts and wildernesses have long been spaces for prayer, meditation and discovery. The natural world helps us rest and discover our purpose.

What is Meditation?

There are plenty of definitions available, but I like to think of meditation as a way of calming a busy mind. Meditation helps you rest in the present moment. The ancient sage Pantanjali taught in his *Yoga Sutras* that the purpose of Yoga is 'to still the fluctuations of the mind'. Many books have been written about precisely what this means, but we can all identify with the discomfort of a busy and distracted mind. Meditation aims to settle the mind. This is an excellent end in itself. Some people also see it as a pathway to union with a higher Reality. Whatever your philosophy and beliefs, you can benefit greatly from meditation.

Meditation and the Senses

Meditation is challenging because your mind is used to being busy. It doesn't always want to settle down. Paying attention to your sensory experience is a good way to calm your over-active thinking. This makes it much easier to settle mindfully into each moment. The natural world offers experiences which engage all your senses. Sounds, sights and sensations all invite you to let go of your mental chatter and simply be. Even a simple natural object like a leaf or a stone has the power to do this. By focusing on nature's gifts you can enjoy the here and now.

Inhaling and Tasting Nature

Begin with your senses of smell and taste. Nature's perfumes engage the emotions. The wild tang of a salt marsh carries the feeling of space and freedom. Few things are lovelier than inhaling the soft, rich scent of a rose. Rubbing aromatic herbs like rosemary or mint between your fingers is a quick route to pleasure. Your nose is tightly tuned to the sweet stink of decay.

Eating mindfully and relishing your food will nourish your body and mind together. Slow and conscious tasting is a meditation in itself. Next time you eat a peach or an orange focus on the sensory experience of the colours, textures and precise flavours. How does each mouthful feel inside your mouth? Allow the burst of sensation to explode and fill your senses. Nature's bounty is here to be experienced to the full.

The Sense of Wonder

A simple blade of grass is wonderful when you look at it carefully. The unique shades of green, fine lines and delicate shapes are remarkable. By challenging yourself to pay more attention to the natural world you can begin to notice its beauty and intricacy. Be fascinated by the spiralling shapes of sunflowers and seashells. If you have a mathematical turn of mind you can meditate on the amazing ways in which the same number patterns repeat themselves throughout the natural universe. Beehives and flower petals, hurricanes and human faces all reflect the same fundamental ratio. We inhabit an amazing world.

Origins and Connections

Another way to meditate on nature is to think about origins and life cycles. Everything tells a story. That blade of grass began as a seed and will one day produce its own seeds. The peach grew on a tree, tended by a farmer, maybe in a distant country. It developed from a blossom, was fertilised by bees and ripened by the sun. The fruit was harvested and travelled a long journey, by ship, lorry and maybe other means of transport. Finally it arrived here in your hand and your mouth. What will happen to its stone? Everything is connected. Even a pebble on a beach has been tossed by the sea, moved and trodden on many times, maybe for thousands of years. What stories would it tell, if it could speak?

Shapes Around the Edges

Sometimes it is interesting to look at the spaces around the edges of things. This is a bit like a drawing exercise where you try to draw the shape of the background instead of focusing on the more obvious object or figure. Notice a line of trees silhouetted against the sky. Then look at the shapes of the sky as it outlines the trees. Instead of looking at the trees, concentrate instead on the gaps between them. What patterns do they make? This can be a different and refreshing way of seeing the world around you.

Sky and Clouds

The sky is full of opportunities for reflection. Why

not spend a while lying down on soft grass and watching the clouds drift past? We all love a gorgeous sunset or a rainbow, but massive cloud formations can be just as fascinating. What pictures can you see? How do the patterns shift and mutate? Maybe you could go outside at night and gaze up at the stars. Or sit on a beach and watch the moon rise over the sea.

Today's Calm Practice: Use your Senses to Meditate on Nature

Take a few minutes today to relax and enjoy a little part of the natural world. Sit quietly with a leaf, a stone or a flower, taking time to appreciate it closely. Use all of your senses to feel, smell, touch and maybe even taste your chosen object. See if it makes a sound when held up to your ear. Does it feel warm or cold, rough or smooth? What happens when you hold it up to the light? What journey has it travelled to reach you here today? How does it make you feel?

Enjoy this piece of nature. Allow it to calm and settle your mind. Be present, here and now.

DAY EIGHTEEN: ENGAGING WITH NATURE

I have always loved searching beaches for interesting stones and fossils. As a little girl I liked to explore rock pools, looking for starfish and sea anenomes. If I am stressed or out of sorts, a stroll by the sea hunting for sharks' teeth and holey stones always makes me feel better. By focusing on the natural world around me I loosen my inner grip on my worries.

Beachcombing is just one way to engage with nature. Spending time doing meaningful activities outdoors is good for your mental and physical health. Even if you live in a city, there are so many opportunities to find calm and happiness by getting involved with the natural world. Some of these can help you make new friends, get active and support your local community. All of them can relieve anxiety or depression and help you feel better.

Growing or Picking Food

Eating something you have grown or harvested yourself is incredibly satisfying. Some people are lucky enough to have gardens or allotments and the time to tend them. But you don't need a lot of space to grow something you can eat. Potatoes in a barrel, strawberries in a hanging basket or cress on the window sill are all fun and delicious. There are lots of great books and websites which can help you get started.

Many local farms offer the chance to pick your own fruit throughout the summer. From strawberries and blackcurrants through to plums and apples you can get involved harvesting your own food. Children love this too. Later in the year I like to pick wild sloes and make my own sloe gin in time for Christmas. For this it is best to wait until after the first frosts when the fruit is tart and full of flavour. Food you have grown or gathered yourself tastes amazing.

With a little information you can find plenty of wild food in the countryside. You might be able to find a local course to learn more about which plants are edible and how to prepare them. If in doubt, stick to what you recognise and know to be safe. August or September is a good time to pick blackberries from the hedgerows. Cook them up with some apples to make a tasty fruit compote or crumble. You may also be able to find mushrooms in the fields, but be careful you know that what you are picking is safe to eat. Check with an expert if you are not sure.

Exercising Outdoors

Exercising outdoors is a brilliant way to keep fit and enjoy your connection to nature. I have already talked about walking and swimming outside. There are plenty of other options too. Whether you prefer running on country trails, paddleboarding on a lake, yoga in a park or flying a kite with the family, you will get all the benefits of being outside in the fresh air. You may make new friends. You will definitely come home with a boost to your health and self-esteem.

The excellent Parkrun organisation is a wonderful way to begin exercising regularly with your local community. You don't have to be able to run - walking is fine too. Everyone is friendly and encouraging. Sadly Parkrun is currently suspended due to Covid 19, but hopefully these accessible events will re-start before too long. Look out for news on their website.

Pets and Wildlife

Many people feel at their most relaxed around animals. Pets and wildlife can encourage you to get outdoors too. If you don't have a pet of your own you could offer to help walk or care for somebody else's. Busy or elderly pet-owners may be very grateful for your input.

There is even an organisation, *Borrow my Doggy*, devoted to helping dog lovers connect with local dog owners for walks, weekends and holidays.

If you enjoy wildlife you could go for a walk in a local park or woodland and look out for birds, deer and other native creatures. Depending on where you live, you might even spot a badger or the elusive red squirrel. You might like to set up bird feeders in your garden and learn about the different species which come to visit. The RSPB website is a great place to start. You could also visit a nature reserve run by the RSPB or your local Wildlife charity. These places are often on the lookout for volunteers, so if you have some spare time you could get involved and help protect local wildlife.

Caring for the Natural World

Caring for your environment is calming and rewarding. It helps you feel more connected to nature. We can all help out by taking part in the 'two minute' movement which encourages everyone to spend two minutes picking up litter when visiting a beach or outdoor space. If you have more time you could get involved in a local litter pick, or help out with conservation projects in your community.

Even big cities have city farms, community gardens and local nature reserves. These are fantastic resources for helping people get close to nature. The Social Farms and Gardens website can help you find green spaces near you. There may be opportunities to volunteer or simply to visit and enjoy.

Stars and the Sky

The night sky is a fascinating way to lose your worries in the natural world. Watching the stars will get you outdoors and encourage you to learn something new. You don't need an expensive telescope to get started. A pair of binoculars or the naked eye is enough to make some great discoveries. All you need is a simple book or two and a clear night. There is plenty of information online about how to get started, and you may be able to find a helpful astronomy club near you. It could be the gateway to a fascinating new hobby.

Eating and Sleeping Outdoors

Picnics and camping are wonderful ways to have fun outdoors in the warmer months. You can put up a tent in your back garden or find a campsite beside a river or in a forest. It is hard to beat the simple pleasure of waking up surrounded by nature, breathing the fresh air and hearing the birds sing. If it rains you can still enjoy the soothing sounds of rain on a tent roof and the cosy feeling of being snuggled up inside. Hopefully the sun will come out again soon!

Today's Calm Practice: Engaging with Nature

Whatever the weather, see if you can find some way today to get involved with the natural world. I have suggested some ideas, but you may think of others too. Perhaps you love gardening or rambling. Maybe you like swimming in the sea. Even something as simple as watching the birds outside your window or tending and watering your houseplants is calming and relaxing. Engaging with nature helps you relate better to yourself and to others. Let the natural world help you feel good today.

DAY NINETEEN: LISTENING MEDITATION

Often my mind is so busy that I do not notice the sounds all around me. I am preoccupied with worries about what I have to do today or the problems in the wider world. But I always feel better when I slow down and and listen to the gentle notes of the wind chimes in my garden. The steady wash of waves on a beach settles my anxieties. When I take time to listen I am soothed by sounds and silence.

Sound is everywhere, inside and out. Your body and and the natural world exist in constant vibration. You can tune in on some of these vibrations by listening to the sounds all around you. Sounds and silence are a wonderful focus for meditation.

A listening meditation is one of my favourite ways to rest my brain. The sense of hearing is powerful and evocative. It can become an anchor for the mind. Focusing on the sounds around around you brings your attention into the present moment. This simple and easy form of meditation is beneficial for your nervous system, concentration skills and long term health.

Sounds and Music for Meditation

Calming music and brainwave frequency sounds are also powerful aids to relaxation and meditation. Many types of music are suitable for helping to soothe the mind. Simple and repetitive sounds are often best as they offer least distraction. Recorded nature sounds or "white noise" can be calming and peaceful.

Some music tracks included embedded brainwave beats. Your brainwaves pulsate at different frequencies depending on whether you are actively thinking, relaxed, meditating or sleeping. The slower brainwave patterns correspond to more restful states of being. Listening to music with brainwave frequency beats can be very helpful for focus, learning, calm or sleep. So-called "binaural beats" are designed to be listened to through headphones as the vibrations are designed to be heard at slightly different frequencies in each ear. You can also enjoy music with monaural or isochronic beats without headphones.

How to Enjoy a Listening Meditation

Start by Closing Your Eyes

To meditate on sounds and silence, simply sit or lie down and close your eyes. You can do this anywhere. You don't have to be in an especially quiet place, although it is best to avoid lots of loud noise, TV or people talking nearby. Take a few deep breaths and begin to relax.

Notice the Sounds Around You

Begin to focus your attention on whatever you can hear around you. Notice all the sounds and noises. Listen intently. If you notice yourself thinking about anything else, gently bring your mind back to whatever you can hear. Keep listening carefully and attentively.

Sounds are not Good or Bad

Allow everything you can hear to enter your ears as a sensory experience. Welcome it all in. Try, just for now, to let go of ideas about certain sounds being good or bad. It is easy to judge birdsong as 'good' and traffic noise as 'bad'. Then before you know it you find yourself thinking about how you must remember to refill the bird feeders, or getting annoyed that they haven't built that bypass yet. You are not aiming to analyse the sounds you can hear. You are simply experiencing sound itself, here and now.

Imagine You have Giant Ears

Sometimes I imagine I have giant ears. This reminds

me that I am living these moments through my sense of hearing. I am allowing my mind to rest on whatever vibrations I detect with my ears. Sound washes over me and through me. I am made of vibrating atoms. I am living in a world of vibrations. Sounds and silence are all around me, inside and out.

Listen to Faraway Sounds

Listen for sounds far away. As far away as you can possibly hear. Maybe you can hear a car three streets away. Perhaps children are playing in the park at the the other end of your road. Can you hear a pigeon walking on the roof? A plane flying high in the sky? The drumming of a woodpecker in the forest? Keep listening.

The Sounds of Your Own Body

Now come close and listen to the sounds deep inside yourself. Can you hear the valves opening and closing inside your heart? Is your stomach gurgling? Listen for the quiet pulsation of the blood behind your eardrums. Can you hear your own breath? Become aware of the sounds of your own remarkable body. These are your most intimate vibrations. Know that you are part of the living and vibrating universe.

The Sound of Silence

Even in a quiet place you will hear many sounds when you begin to listen. Can you hear the sound of silence? Among the birdsong, the bees, the footsteps and the grasshoppers, are there moments of stillness? Perhaps you begin to detect rhythms and moments of rest. Listen for silence, and allow yourself to experience this too. What does silence sound like?

Return Slowly

When you have finished listening, take some time simply to rest. Then slowly begin to become aware of your surroundings again. Begin gradually to move your body. Enjoy some deeper breaths as you wriggle and stretch your fingers and toes, your arms and legs. Take a few moments to relax and notice how you feel before continuing with your day.

Today's Calm Practice: Listening Meditation

Take ten minutes today to relax and listen to all the sounds around you. Focus all your attention on whatever you hear, without judgement or thinking too much. Let the sounds envelop you and enjoy the experience.

CREATIVITY

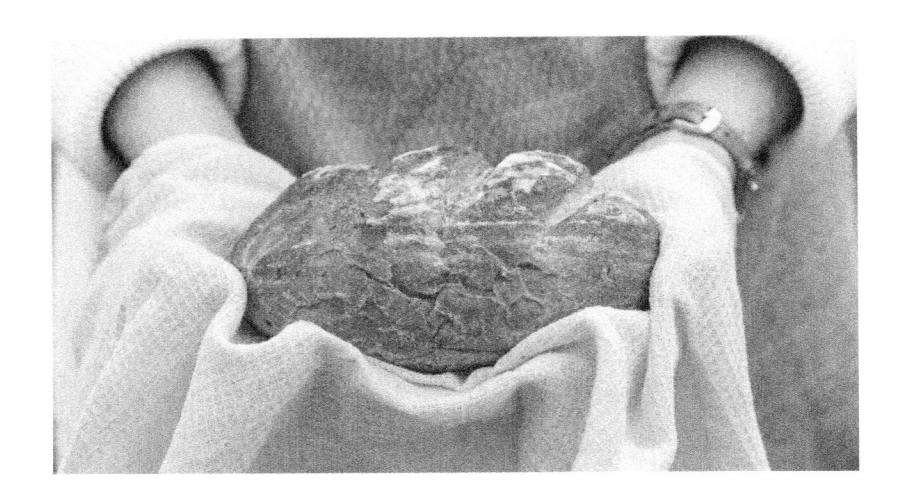

DAY TWENTY: BAKING BREAD

In the first weeks of lockdown in Spring 2020 it was virtually impossible to buy yeast for baking. Flour was hard to come by too. This was partly due to perceived food shortages, but mostly because people were turning to traditional home baking as a grounding and calming activity. Humans have an innate drive to create. Baking bread and cakes became a creative safe haven in an uncertain world.

Baking bread is soothing and calming. At the end you have something delicious to share and eat. It is a great way to care for yourself and others.

A Feast for the Senses

Making your own bread is a feast for the senses. From starting the yeast culture through to munching a tasty slice still warm from the oven, the whole process is intensely satisfying. It connects us with memories of our grandparents and ancestors. I love the smell of the yeast and the ceremony of mixing it with warm water and sugar to wake into bubbly life. Stirring this culture into warm flour, I am creating something new right here in my kitchen.

Then comes the kneading. Squeezing and pounding the dough, my inner child gets a chance to play. I am three years old again and exploring new sensations. I like the patterns my knuckles makes in the springy dough. If I am feeling cross or frustrated I can bang and slap it around most satisfyingly. Kneading is a brilliant meditation for the hands. The mixture slowly becomes stretchy and shiny, changing in texture at my touch. When it is well-pounded and smooth, I nestle my dough in a bowl, cover it, and leave it in a warm place to prove.

Baking Bread Takes Time

Baking bread with yeast is a natural process. It takes time. It is an invitation to slow down your frantic pace of life. While the yeast quietly multiplies in your dough you might like to go out for a walk or take a relaxing bath. There is no hurry and you can return to it when you are ready. There is plenty of time to breathe and reflect.

Baking is a beautiful teacher of patience and the peaceful pace of growth.

Getting Creative

Most recipes now tell you to knock the excess air out of your dough and knead it again. Now you can decide what shape you would like your bread to be. You might choose a traditional loaf tin or a clay flower pot. You could make your bread into rolls or a round cottage loaf. If you are feeling especially creative you can experiment with plaits, animal shapes or other artistry. It's up to you. Get creative and have fun.

Wonderful Aromas

Once your bread has had more time to prove and double in size you can put it in a hot oven. Delicious aromas begin to fill the house. The smell is irresistible. Everyone looks forward to munching on a steaming slice dripping with butter and maybe some jam. Before long you will be ready to taste and share your creation. If you have children they will soon demolish your work. If you have made an extra loaf you could share this with a neighbour.

Bringing People Together

Baking and sharing bread brings people together. For millennia, families and communities have gathered to 'break bread' around simple and wholesome meals. Sometimes this takes on a spiritual significance. In Jewish family and community life the blessing, breaking and sharing of the challah loaves at the Shabbat meal is a key expression of faith. For others, cooking and eating with family or friends can be a treasured time for connection.

International Bake Bread for Peace Day

October 24th is International Bake Bread for Peace Day. In 2014, an Irish lady called Breezy Willow Kelly in County Donegal was feeling saddened by all the conflict and sorrow in the world. Breezy started encouraging individuals and communities to come together and share their desire for world peace through the ancient and peaceful activity of baking and sharing bread. What a beautiful idea! You can learn more about Breezy and follow her inspiring Facebook page at https://www.facebook.com/bakebreadforpeace

Different Types of Bread

There are many different ways to bake bread. As well as traditional white or wholemeal yeast breads you can try sourdough (where you nurture your own wild yeast culture), quick soda breads, or gluten free recipes. You can add cheese or olives, eggs or sugar to make delicious speciality breads. Brioche and ciabatta, rye bread and focaccia are all glorious ways to play with dough. A world of creativity awaits.

Baking Bread and Calm

Simple and practical activities are calming to the nervous system. You can absorb yourself and forget your worries in playful sensory experiences where not too much is at stake. If your bread burns or fails to rise that is no great disaster. You have enjoyed the journey and hopefully learned something for next time. It is a gentle lesson in coping with imperfection.

Today's Calming Practice - Baking Bread

Why not have a try at baking some bread today? This is a great activity to share with children. Alternatively you may prefer the peace of doing it on your own. Think about who might like to eat your bread too. Could you take some to a lonely or elderly neighbour?

The link below will take you to a simple recipe for a traditional white loaf. If you prefer you can find plenty of alternative options online, including gluten free and vegan breads. The BBC Good Food website is a great place to start. Or maybe you have a favourite family recipe. The main thing is to have a go, relax and enjoy the experience. Delicious!

https://www.bbcgoodfood.com/recipes/classic-white-loaf

DAY TWENTY-ONE: JOURNALING FOR CALM

During the lockdown in the spring of 2020 I sat down every morning to write three longhand pages in my journal. This was my safe space. I could download my worries, frustrations and anxieties onto uncomplaining paper. I placed no fixed structure or particular demands on my writing. I simply had to fill three pages. This journaling practice helped me cope with stress and uncertainty. It allowed me to process my thoughts, play with ideas and begin each day in quiet reflection. It was a lifeline.

Journaling for Calm and Creativity

Many therapists and mental health professionals recommend the practice of journaling. Writing down your thoughts each day is helpful for depression, anxiety and managing stress. Daily journaling can bring calm, focus and direction into your life. People report that keeping a journal enables them to be more grateful, more productive, more creative and happier. Journaling helps me discover and focus on my life goals. It is an outlet for negative emotions and a liberating place to develop new ideas.

No Fixed Rules

There are no fixed rules about what or how to write. Your journal is your private space. You can relax and be yourself here. There are probably as many ways to journal as there are individuals.

Having said that, it is often helpful to have a framework for beginning or refreshing a daily journaling habit. Here are some ideas to help you get started.

Choose a Regular Time and Place - and Stick to It!

Journaling is most powerful when it is practised on a regular daily basis. Tiny habits have a huge impact. Little things, practiced daily, can massively improve your life.

It is much easier to stick to any daily practice if you

do it at the same time and place every day. Have a think about when journaling could fit into your life. Just ten minutes each day can be enough to make a difference. If you have a bit longer, that's even better. Try to find a time when you can be undisturbed for a little while. First thing in the morning often works well. You can start your day's activities feeling calm and focused. Or maybe you are not a morning person? The evening is a good time too. You can use your journal to reflect on the day and maybe plan for tomorrow.

It also helps to have a dedicated place for your journaling. This might be your bedroom, the garden shed or the kitchen table. Anywhere you can sit quietly each day to write. If possible, keep your journal and pens here (but make sure they are safe from prying eyes too!). Our brains build stronger habits when we learn to associate an activity with a specific location and daily routine. For example, when I finish clearing up breakfast, I get out my journal, sit by the window and write.

Choose a Dedicated Notebook and Pen (or Pens!)

I tend to journal much more regularly when I use a book that I like. This is very much a question of personal taste, but I recommend you give it some thought. My preference is for an A5 size notebook with an attractive cover, rounded corners to the paper, dots in a grid pattern instead of lines on the pages, and an elastic thingy to hold the pages closed. You might prefer a big A4 book, or something smaller. What matters is that you feel good about the book you choose. It should feel a bit special and make you want to write in it. On the other hand, don't buy a book so beautiful that you feel afraid to sully it with your scribblings. Your journal is your space to be yourself, warts and all.

Pens matter too. I like to use lots of colours depending on my mood, so I have a jar full of fine line coloured pens. Some people like an old fashioned fountain pen. Others go for a pot full of simple ballpens or pencils. Having a pen or pens at the ready makes me feel like the sort of person who journals. And I don't want to waste my precious journaling time searching the house for a pen.

Digital Journaling Apps

Some people like to use digital journaling apps. I prefer the release of writing stuff down longhand on paper, but apps can offer other features like daily prompts and the ability to add photos. If you are interested in exploring this option further I have added a link below to a useful review of apps currently on offer.

What to Write

So now you are sitting down in a quiet space with your journal and pen. What are you going to write? You can simply take a free flow approach, writing down your thoughts as they arise. Alternatively if you like structure and some ideas to get you started, journaling prompts are often very useful. You can try different approaches and see what works for you.

Freeform Daily Pages

With this approach you decide how much paper you want to cover and then just go for it. Your only goal is to fill a certain amount of space, writing longhand, each day. This works best if you have at least twenty minutes set aside for your journaling. You can write whatever you like. I often start out by having a good moan about whatever is bothering me. Once I have got this out of my system I generally find I can be more positive, creative and hopeful. The simple process of writing down whatever comes to mind is remarkably calming and freeing.

Remember that your writing does not have to be 'good' in any sense. It is whatever comes. This is your space. Think of it as a playground. Do whatever you like with it. The benefits are huge.

This freeform journaling style is taught by Julia Cameron in her inspirational book, *'The Artist's Way'*. Check out the book if this appeals to you. You don't have to be an artist to use it!

Structured Prompts

You might prefer to try a more structured form of journaling. Sit down with your journal and ask yourself the same questions every day:

- *What do I really need, right here and now?*

- *What do I need to do today to meet these immediate needs?*

- *Writing in the present tense, what does my ideal day look like, as I imagine it today?*
- *What three things am I grateful for today?*

- *How would I like my life to look three years from now?*

- *What one action can I commit to doing today that will bring me a tiny step closer to my ideal life?*

Write down your daily thoughts in response to each question. If you are short of time, just choose two or three questions each day. Ideally keep doing this for a month or longer. You can combine it with setting meaningful goals each month too, if you wish. You will begin to see positive changes in your life.

I have found this journaling style to be an incredibly powerful tool for personal growth. It helps me focus every day on what is genuinely important for my well-being. It keeps me thankful and proactive in looking after myself and others. Journaling and self-care go hand in hand.

Keep it Fresh

Consistency is a big part of journaling. But after some time you can become tired of a particular journaling style. I usually notice this has happened when my journal degenerates into a 'To Do List'. Maybe I am writing the same things every day. My journal has become a chore instead of a liberation. Then it is time to try a fresh approach. You could try writing freeform for a change and see how that feels. Or try some different prompts to inspire you and shake things up.

Other Types of Prompts

There are lots of journaling prompts you can use to refresh or inspire your daily writing. Some focus more on self-care. Others are useful for productivity, positive mood or self-discovery. You can search online for journaling prompts. Find something that makes you want to start writing and then go for it.

No one has to Read It

Remember that no one has to read your journal. Not even you, unless you want to! The process of writing stuff down is the important bit. It is a journey of release and self-discovery. Feel free to write 'badly', unload all your rubbish and be yourself. You are not trying to create a work of literature. Your journal is your private space. It is your playground and your rubbish dump. It is your space. It belongs to you and no one else.

Today's Calming Practice: Journaling

Find a notebook and pen. Sit down somewhere quiet for fifteen to twenty minutes and write. You can use prompts if you like, or just see what comes. You don't have to read your writing back unless you want to. Experience writing your thoughts down on paper. Remember, it doesn't have to be good. Simply write. Then stop and take a few moments to notice how you feel.

#

DAY TWENTY-TWO: CRAFTING AND CREATIVITY

I always enjoy working on my crochet or knitting when watching television in the evening. The simple repetitive process of hooking coloured wool helps me relax at the end of a busy day. It keeps me in a settled state of mind and stops me slumping into unconsciousness on the sofa. Keeping my hands occupied doing someone creative has a calming effect on my brain. The pleasure of creative crafts is first and foremost about the process. The finished product is an added bonus.

You can create and craft your calm space with crochet, colour or macrame. There are so many soothing and accessible ways to access your natural creativity.

Crafting is Good for You

There is lots of research evidence showing that simple, repetitive crafts like knitting and crochet are good for your health. The experience of repeatedly making precise hand movements has similar effects on the brain to meditation. Knitting has been shown to lower the heart rate and wake up the calming parasympathetic nervous system. Crafts like crochet, spinning, sewing or decoupage can lower your blood pressure and help you release tension, improving long term health. They can have the same relaxing benefits as gentle Yoga or breathing exercises.

When you create and craft you use both hemispheres of the brain. Your imaginative right brain and your steady, practical left brain work together in balanced harmony. You remain alert yet relaxed all at the same time. This explains why you can knit in front of the television late into the evening without falling asleep!

Finding Your Flow

Much has been written in recent years about the concept of flow. Flow is the effortless concentration and enjoyment you find when you are wholly absorbed in an activity. It happens when you complete a task and realise you have lost all track of time. You have let go of all other concerns and become entirely present to your occupation. It is a calm and productive experience. Meditation, writing, meaningful work and crochet can all take you to this peaceful place.

Everyone is Creative

Creativity is not confined to a few special people. Everyone is creative. Children love to make imaginative new worlds as they play. Yoga philosophy teaches the concept of the chakras. These are energy centres within the body, sometimes visualised as spinning wheels. The sacral chakra deep within the pelvis is believed to be the source of sexuality and creativity. These drives are fundamental to human life.

Everyone has natural creative energy. Sometimes this energy might be blocked or buried. Perhaps you were discouraged from making or drawing things in childhood. Maybe someone told you you were not 'good at art', or that it was a waste of time. Maybe the focus was too much on achievement and not enough on playful expression. Many people feel intimidated or bored by crafts, but there are so many ways to express your inner artistry. Letting go of the need to make something 'good' can free you to enjoy the experience.

Find a Good Teacher and Make New Friends

Learning a new craft can build your self-esteem and confidence. It is also a great way to bond with family members of make new friends. Learning to sew patchwork or knit from your mother or auntie is a beautiful way to pass down family skills. Alternatively you can find a local tutor or class. Maybe you have always fancied having a go at pottery, weaving or life drawing. There is probably a class near you. Some people discover a whole new community through crafting. These groups are wonderful for building friendships and supporting mental health.

In these times of pandemic some face-to-face classes may sadly be suspended. However you can still find plenty of craft tuition and support online. Maybe your local college or arts centre is offering online courses? Or you could join an inspiring group from further afield. A little research can point you to some wonderful new opportunities to learn and support your wellbeing.

Woolly Crafts

Making things with wool is incredibly calming. Our ancestors have been working with natural fibres for many thousands of years. As well as knitting and crochet, woolly crafts include weaving, spinning, felt making and more. These are all lovely ways to engage with colour and texture. Once you have the basic techniques you can release your imagination to make whatever takes your fancy.

Learning a new skill can be a fun and liberating experience. A few years ago I watched someone working at a spinning wheel. I was instantly fascinated by the soothing rhythm. I found a teacher, bought a second hand wheel on eBay and had a go for myself. So far I have produced only some very lumpy and uneven yarn, but I have had a wonderful time playfully learning. Feeling part of the whole process from sheep to knitted pot-holder is deeply satisfying.

Create and Craft in Other Ways

Maybe knitting or crochet is not your thing. There are plenty of other ways to express your creativity. Painting or drawing, flower arranging or cake decorating are all just as enjoyable whether you are an accomplished expert or a complete beginner. You might be a gardener, stone-balancer or brick-layer. You could learn to use a sewing machine or make patchwork by hand. Or try pebble painting, making a scrapbook, origami or macrame ... the important thing is to find something that appeals and give it a go.

Keep it Simple

Creativity doesn't have to be daunting. For your wellbeing, the main thing is to absorb yourself in the experience. Begin with something easy. Complex colouring books, jigsaw puzzles and painting by numbers are all beautiful mindful activities. These are great ways to relax and calm a busy mind. You don't need to impress anybody. No one is expecting you to produce the Mona Lisa! Allow a creative activity to become your playground. If you enjoy doing it, you are doing it right.

Today's Calm Practice: Get Creative

Spend at least thirty mins today absorbing yourself in something crafty or creative. Think of this as a relaxing meditation. The finished product doesn't matter. Get out your old knitting, or find a colouring book or a puzzle. You might even like to research learning a new craft. If you want to keep it simple, you can find lots of lovely free designs for adult colouring online. Relax and enjoy the experience.

#

DAY TWENTY-THREE: HAIKU

'**N**o one travels
 Along this way but I
 This autumn evening.'

- *Matsuo Basho, 1644-1694*

Haiku is a Japanese poetic form closely tied to meditation. Classical haiku are works of genius. Many of them were penned by Zen monks. Their beauty lies in their beguiling simplicity. Reading and contemplating haiku opens and frees the mind.

I love and admire the work of Basho, Issa, Buson and the great Haiku masters. In my own small way I also like to compose haiku. Anyone can write their own haiku as a personal meditative practice. They

do not have to be brilliant. My little productions compare poorly with the precise and haunting beauty of the masters' work. But the process is powerful. The experience of composition focuses the mind and heart. It feels like solving a particularly satisfying puzzle.

Small, Precise and Beautiful

Small, precise and beautiful, a haiku evokes emotion, usually by making reference to nature. A haiku poet observes the detail of the world around with loving attention. Her or his words encapsulate a sliver of experience, awaking awe, surprise or recognition in the reader. Sometimes there is a surprise in the juxtaposition of images or ideas. Like all poetry, haiku aims to communicate something real with felt accuracy. It can be sad, happy, funny, or simply an observation. A good haiku is worth long and slow consideration.

Three Short Lines

A haiku usually has three short lines. Traditionally there are seventeen syllables, with a 5-7-5 structure. A haiku doesn't usually rhyme. Some excellent writers maintain that the 5-7-5 pattern is not required in English. It is sufficient to create a concise three line poem. I enjoy the constraint of the syllable count when I compose haiku as it makes the construction more challenging. I can't simply use the first phrases that spring to mind, as I have to search for other forms to fit the syllables. This encourages me to play with words as I attempt to express my idea. It is a small creative conundrum.

Poetry and Meditation

We are creatures who naturally use language. Words can confuse and hurt us, but they also have the power to calm, centre and soothe. Poetry, scriptures and mantras have been used for centuries in meditation to focus and settle the mind. I regularly read poetry aloud to my students at the end of my Yoga classes to facilitate contemplative relaxation.

When you read or hear a poem you don't have to struggle to understand everything. Allow the words to wash over you like water and enjoy the images that settle in your imagination. Poetry can paint a picture or leave you with a resounding word or phrase. Let that become the focus for your meditation. The word or picture that feels meaningful for you is like a delicious sweet in your mouth. Enjoy it, explore it and let it linger. Relax into it.

Composing Poetry

Writing your own haiku or poetry can be a private expression for you alone. Don't worry about whether or not it is 'good'. Try playing with words in the same way that you might experiment with fitting pieces into a jigsaw puzzle. It is like testing different shades of paint on a wall, or trying on clothes looking for the perfect outfit. There is no right or wrong way to do it. The experience of finding words for this moment in time is a meditation in itself.

Writing down your poems, maybe in a special notebook, is a lovely way to keep a record of your feelings and experiences. You can do this simply for yourself as a private treasure trove.

Of course you might like to write poems to share with others. This can become a deeply absorbing hobby. You might even like to join a writing group or share your work online. But don't discount the liberating experience of composition purely for pleasure too.

Nature, Walks and Moods

Nature has moods, and so do we. I like trying to compose haiku when I am out walking. It is a little challenge that encourages me to notice details in my environment and how they make me feel. Finding words for my experience of nature on this particular day focuses my mind and imagination. It turns my walk into a meditation. If I am feeling low or agitated, thinking about my haiku lifts my mood and calms me. It is especially helpful in times of stress and during pandemic lockdown periods.

A Couple of My Attempts

With apologies to Basho, here are a couple of my recent haiku attempts:

Ferns stand head high now
Unfurled to herald summer
You can't lock them down.

— *3 June 2020*

Walking the seawall
Sky maze on purple salt marsh

A landward rainbow.

- 21 August 2020

Work of a Master

And here is one from another great master:

*'The light of a candle
Is transferred to another candle -
Spring twilight.'*

- Yosa Buson, 1716 - 1784

Today's Calming Practice - Write a Haiku

Have a go at composing a haiku today. It usually helps to go outside or look closely at something from nature. When your attention is drawn to something, notice exactly how it appears to your senses. What feeling, thoughts and emotions does it evoke for you?

Now try to write three short lines which describe your experience. You can choose whether or not to stick to the 5-7-5 syllable count. Don't worry about what anyone else would think of your haiku. Just take time to put your own meditation into words. Notice how this makes you feel.

CONNECTION

DAY TWENTY-FOUR: GRATITUDE

When my seven children were younger I often felt overwhelmed by the constant demands of working and caring for my family. One day someone suggested a different way to think about my daily tasks. When something seems irksome or difficult, you can choose instead to see it as a gift. In this way even the most annoying jobs can become an opportunity for gratitude.

Apply Gratitude to Daily Tasks

Instead of thinking: 'I have to go shopping for food', I choose to think: 'I can go shopping for food at a full supermarket. I have sufficient recourses to feed my family. I am so grateful I can do this.'

Instead of thinking: 'I have to get the children ready in time for school', I choose to think: 'I have healthy children. They have the opportunity to go to school and get an education. I am so grateful.'

Instead of thinking: 'I have to get some exercise to keep fit', I can think: 'I have arms and legs that work and the ability to exercise. Many people do not have this. Exercising might be tough but I know I will feel better for it. I am so grateful.'

Instead of thinking, 'I have to do all this laundry and ironing', I can think: 'I have clothes and all the clean water and equipment I need to keep them clean. This is a wonderful gift.'

This grateful approach can be applied to virtually any task. I don't always remember to think like this, but when I do I feel so much better.

Benefits of Gratitude

The benefits of gratitude are enormous. Developing daily habits of gratitude changes your brain and personality in wonderfully positive ways. Research evidence shows that gratitude will make you happier, healthier and more productive. People who practice gratitude regularly consistently report marked improvements in their relationships, careers and emotions. A better marriage, stronger immune system, more sleep, increased self-esteem and happier memories are just some of the gifts of gratitude. Gratitude is good for you. It is well worth cultivating!

Negativity Comes Naturally

You probably find that you often focus on problems and worries. This is normal. Don't waste energy feeling guilty about negative thinking. Human beings are biologically predisposed to focus on negative ideas and outcomes. This goes back to our prehistoric ancestors who needed rapidly to envisage the worst possible outcomes in order to survive in a dangerous world. Today most of us do not live under immediate threat from wild predators or attackers. Yet we still tend to focus on disaster scenarios and what is lacking. This attitude may sometimes be useful, but much of the time it is detrimental to your health and happiness. You will feel better and become more productive when you develop more positive habits of thought.

Don't Wallow in Guilt - Be Generous Instead

Lets not confuse gratitude with feeling pointlessly guilty that we have more than others. I may reflect with gratitude that I have plenty to eat while many in the world go hungry. These thoughts may lead me to greater generosity to those in need. I may become a kinder and more caring person. But once I have done what I can for others I should still be happy that I have what I need. Allowing guilt to destroy the gifts of gratitude helps no one. Instead try to let gratitude and the feelings of freedom and wellbeing that flow from it become a source of generosity.

Keeping a Gratitude Journal

Keeping a gratitude journal is a great way to get into the habit of feeling grateful. Each day write down three things you feel grateful for. Spend a few minutes thinking about those things. What difference do they make to your life? How do they make you feel? How is your life better as a result?

Once you start thinking about it, there are so many things to be grateful for. You might be thankful for people or animals who make a difference in your life. Maybe you notice the joys of this moment - the feeling of the sun on your skin, or the way light reflects on water. Daily food, fresh air and health are natural sources of gratitude. Perhaps you are grateful for aspects of your community, your home or your faith. Once you begin to practice gratitude you will start to notice more and more gifts all around you.

Other Ways to Practice Gratitude

Gratitude is a great habit to cultivate. It is wonderful to build it into your life on a regular basis. If journaling doesn't appeal to you, you could try spending a few minutes at the end of each day reflecting on what went well today. You might like to share your grateful thoughts with a family member or a friend. Or you can just think about them as you settle down for sleep. Gratitude can help you sleep better and wake feeling positive.

Today I am Grateful ...

For a rainy day, giving me time to catch up on my writing.

For my loving family and opportunities to spend time with them.

For the local swimming pool where I started my day with a refreshing swim.

Today's Calm Practice: Gratitude Reflection

Sit quietly for ten minutes and write down three things you feel grateful for right now. Reflect on how these things make you feel good. Be grateful. Notice how gratitude feels inside your body. Enjoy the feeling.

If you wish, share something you are grateful for with someone else. You might like to thank someone who supports you and tell them how much you appreciate them. This way you can share the benefits of gratitude and make the world a better place.

DAY TWENTY-FIVE: LOVING KINDNESS

I am always humbled when I hear about people who forgive in the face of devastating wrong. This is one of the most impressive human feats. I recently read about a former work colleague whose son was stabbed to death only days after her husband had died from Covid 19. This remarkable woman was able publicly to declare her forgiveness for her son's killers. Knowing her to be a person of kindness and integrity, I realised that her ability to forgive was consistent with her profound faith and goodness. My sorrow at her terrible loss mingled with admiration. I asked myself: could I do that?

The Cost of Holding onto Anger

Humans are social creatures. Your relationships play a big part in your happiness. Most religions and philosophies give an important place to loving relationships. It is relatively easy to be kind to people you naturally like, but you are inevitably confronted with difficult people too. The way you relate to others is crucial for your inner peace.

'Holding onto anger is like grasping a hot coal with the intent of throwing it at somebody else: you are the one who gets burned.' These words of wisdom are often attributed to the Buddha. Whatever their origin, the meaning is clear. Anger, bitterness and failing to forgive is seriously harmful. Jesus taught that we should forgive those who wrong us and even love our enemies. Sometimes this seems impossible, but the inability to forgive causes ongoing damage.

Forgiveness, Science and Health

Modern science agrees with the teaching of faith traditions that forgiveness and loving relationships are crucial for our wellbeing. Research studies show that people who are able to forgive wrongs have lower levels of depression and anxiety and better mental health. They also have a higher white blood cell count which is a key component of the immune system. This means they are less likely to contract infections. Forgiveness is also related to better parenting skills and increased self-esteem. Another study showed that chronically angry people have higher levels of heart disease and worse disease outcomes. Holding onto anger can actually kill you.

Loving Relationships and Dealing with Hurt

Fortunately we do not all suffer the murder of loved ones. But we all have to deal with difficult people and challenging relationships. Bosses at work, spouses, in-laws, colleagues or even passers-by can upset us and cause us pain. Finding ways of coping when people hurt us is essential for our inner peace.

If other people are causing you ongoing stress then I encourage you to look for ways to heal the problem. The approach will depend on the severity of the issue and the nature of the relationship. An encounter with an enraged road user whom you will probably never see again can be very disturbing. But its impact is very different from the ongoing damage caused by an abusive partner or a bullying boss.

Professional Help and Counselling

If a relationship is causing you serious problems then it is important to get the right sort of help and support, especially if you feel the relationship has become abusive. You can talk to a trusted friend or a health professional. You can also seek counselling from a qualified therapist or reputable organisation. Sometimes counselling can positively transform a struggling relationship. Sometimes, sadly, you might need to end a relationship or leave a job to protect your health and wellbeing. A friend or counsellor may be able to help you discern this. I have included a few links to useful organisations in

Links and Further Reading at the end of this book.

You must always tell someone - a health professional, teacher, police officer or social worker - if you think a child is at risk of harm.

Transforming Difficult Feelings

Some situations may be less intense but still difficult. Maybe you are not actively being hurt but you are left with painful feelings about an encounter or a relationship. Even though you may never meet the person again, or they do not play a big part in your life, feelings of bitterness or anger can linger. This is when meditation, prayer and mindful practices can really help. You have the ability to transform your painful emotions. Often this can take some time, and sometimes you will need the support of other people. But it is most definitely possible and highly worthwhile.

Meditative and Mindful Practices

Many of the meditative and calming practices covered in this book are helpful for dealing with anger and painful emotions. Gentle Yoga, breath meditation, walking in nature and journaling are all wonderful ways to calm the body and mind. When you let go of anxiety and focus on the present moment you can effortlessly loosen painful memories and calm bitter feelings.

Three Step Rewind and Hypnotherapy

The Three Step Rewind process is very effective for dealing with difficult memories and emotions. This is a safe guided relaxation which enables you to lay to rest patterns of thought which no longer serve you. The Rewind is based on Neurolinguistic Programming (NLP). It is simple and effective. I am a trained Three Step Rewind practitioner, and I have included a link to more information in *Links and Further Reading* if you would like to learn more about this.

Hypnotherapy can also be a powerful way to deal with anger and anxiety. Look for a fully qualified professional if you would like to explore this.

Loving Kindness Meditation

The Loving Kindness Meditation or *metta bhavana* from the Buddhist tradition is a beautiful way to cultivate loving feelings towards ourselves and others. Regular practice of this meditation will soften bitter feelings and help you develop healthier and more positive relationships.

It is impossible to feel love and kindness towards other people if we are unable to love ourselves. We need first to understand what love feels like. The Loving Kindness Meditation practice builds on this crucial understanding.

The practice then goes on to focus on feeling love and kindness towards other people - first those we like, and then others. Here is how to do it:

Begin by sitting quietly, relaxing and focusing on your breathing. Make sure you feel settled and safe.

Feeling Safe and Loved

Recall a time and place when you felt completely safe and loved. Maybe you can imagine being with a close friend, a child or a beloved pet. Perhaps you have a happy memory from your childhood. Focus all your attention on experiencing the warm feeling of being loved, cared for and appreciated. Allow yourself to feel safe and loved. Take some time to enjoy this feeling. Send yourself kind and loving thoughts.

Some people find this difficult. If so, then stop here. Each time you practice the Loving Kindness meditation, focus on sending yourself feelings of being loved. You could simply repeat to yourself, 'I am loved.'

Send Love to a Loved One

When you are comfortably able to feel love for yourself, begin to think of a person you find easy to love. Maybe you have a special friend, a beloved family member or a wonderful pet. Visualise that person in front of you. In your mind send them the same warm feelings of love and kindness you have felt towards yourself. See this person relaxing and smiling as your love reaches them. Enjoy the feeling of sending love to a loved one.

Send Love to Someone Else

This may be enough. But if you feel able, you can move onto imagining a person towards whom your feelings are neutral. This might be a work colleague, someone you have seen at a shop or cafe, or any real person you neither especially like nor dislike. Visualise this person standing in front of you, and practice sending loving thoughts to them. Imagine them softening and smiling. Notice how you feel.

A Person You Find Difficult

Only when you feel able, you can extend the practice to a person you find difficult. It is best to start with someone you find slightly irritating rather than the awful boss who terrorises you. You can gradually build up to that person. Just as before, visualise the difficult person standing in front of you. See if you can send kind and loving thoughts to them. Focus on their wellbeing. In your imagination send them kindness and all the good things they need.

Afterwards, come back to yourself again. Feel that warm sense of being loved. Send yourself some more love and kindness.

Now relax. Allow your mind and emotions to be free. Take some time to just breathe and rest. When you are ready, finish your meditation and continue with your day.

Different Ways to Practice

There are different ways to practice the Loving Kindness Meditation. You can focus solely on yourself and feelings of love. Or you can extend the practice to feeling love towards the whole Universe and all living beings. Do what feels safe and comfortable for you. Everyone has different needs and experiences. Don't feel bad if you struggle with this practice at first. Just take it slowly and gently. Regular practice is powerful.

Loving Kindness Mantra

It can be helpful to use a simple mantra. Try repeating the following phrases in your mind as you focus on each person:

'May you be well.
May you be safe.
May you be happy.'

Taking it into the World

Notice how you feel towards the people in your meditation when you meet them in the real world. Maybe you find yourself giving a smile to that person in the supermarket, or sending a card to a friend who needs cheering up. The Loving Kindness meditation can make a real difference to your life and relationships.

Today's Calm Practice: Loving Kindness

You might like to try the Loving Kindness meditation today. Sit quietly and focus on feeling loving kindness towards yourself. Extend that feeling to others if you feel able.

See if you can do something kind for somebody today. Give someone a card or a small gift to tell them you care. Send your kind thoughts or prayers to someone who needs them. Smile at a stranger. Remember to care for yourself too.

DAY TWENTY-SIX: MANTRA MEDITATION

I am a big fan of Kundalini Yoga. This beautiful practice involves lots of mantra repetition and chanting, often combined with movements. I find that the chanting gives me energy and focus, with a wonderful sense of calm afterwards. I often use a mantra or repeated phrase in my personal prayer times. Sometimes life is challenging and I struggle to find words of my own. Praying the rosary or meditating with prayer beads is especially supportive at times like this.

A Tool for the Mind

The word *mantra* is derived from two Sanskrit words: *manas*, meaning mind, and *tra,* meaning tool. A mantra is a tool for the mind - a help for anyone seeking to settle the mind or access higher connections and levels of consciousness.

Contrary to common belief meditation does not require you to empty your mind. Your mind naturally thinks. It is virtually impossible to stop the thought process altogether. A mantra gives your mind something to do. There are many ways to meditate. You can focus on the breath, on sensory experience or on a mantra. These are all ways of occupying the mind in a simple activity. The mantra or other focus settles your thoughts and calms over-stimulated electrical activity in your brain.

Mantra Meditation and Science

Mantras have been used in many faith traditions for thousands of years. Today they are often recommended in modern secular mindfulness practice. Scientific research confirms the value of mantra meditation for health and wellbeing. People practising meditation using a mantra were shown in controlled research studies to be more relaxed and and to have less distracted brain activity. The meditative repetition of a positive or calming phrase can induce deep relaxation and can even have self-hypnotic effects.

Sanskrit Mantras

Mantras are used widely in Yogic and Hindu traditions. Many people believe that the Sanskrit language is especially spiritual and that the vibrations of Sanskrit phrases carry transformative power. The sacred syllable *Om* or *Aum* is believed to be the essential vibration of the Universe. By chanting *Om*, Yogis seek to align themselves with this eternal reality.

Other popular Sanskrit phrases for mantra meditation include *Sat Nam*, meaning 'truth is my identity' and *Om Shanti*, which is an invocation for peace. *Om Mani Padme Hum* literally means 'the jewel of the lotus'. This refers to the spiritual path of wisdom which leads to enlightenment.

Mantras in Other Traditions

Many faith traditions use the repetition of words or short phrases in prayer and contemplation. Muslims repeat the name *Allah* or meditate on short phrases from the Qur'an. Jews recite *Barukh ahah Adonai* ('Blessed art thou, O Lord'). Christians in the Eastern traditions pray the Jesus prayer, *'Lord Jesus Christ, Son of God, have mercy on me a sinner'*. Catholic Christians pray the *Hail Mary* on rosary beads.

Malas, Beads and Knotted Ropes

Beads or knotted ropes are used across many traditions to accompany mantra meditations and prayers. Buddhist mala beads usually consist of 108 beads plus one guru bead. The beads are held and fingered in meditation, with one bead being counted for each repetition of the mantra. 108 is a sacred number in Buddhism.

Other faiths also use rosaries, *misbaha* or knotted

prayer ropes as an aid to mantra meditation or prayer. Prayer beads have been identified in ancient art dating back as far as the seventeenth century BC. Humans are clearly drawn to using beads for meditation. The tactile experience of handling the beads is soothing and quickly comes to be associated with a contemplative and calm state of mind. The beads or knots also serve the practical purpose of counting the repetitions of the mantra.

Mudras

Mantra meditation is sometimes combined with the use of mudras. A mudra is a hand position or movement believed to affect energy flows in the body and mind. There are many mudras for many different purposes. A popular one is Gyan Mudra where the thumbs and index fingers are lightly touched together on both hands, with palms open. This is thought to be conducive to meditation and wisdom. Like beads, special hand positions can help you enter a state of calm and mental quiet.

You Don't Have to be Religious

Anyone can benefit from mantra meditation, whether or not you follow a faith or tradition. A mantra can be any word or phrase, in any language, that you find helpful or meaningful. You might like to use a traditional Sanskrit mantra or one from your faith tradition. Or you may prefer to use a helpful phrase in English or your own language. It can be anything that inspires and supports you. The main thing is to feel comfortable with the mantra you choose.

Mantras for Sport, Birth or Challenging Times

Mantras can help us keep going through difficult challenges. Athletes and marathon runners encourage themselves by repeating phrases like, 'light and smooth', 'keep moving forwards', or 'eat my shorts' (my husband's favourite!). For the adventure of birthing, a mother might breathe 'open', 'I am strong', or 'yes I can' as each surge brings her baby closer. A mantra is a powerful affirmation of purpose and identity. It reminds us who we are.

Choosing a Mantra

A good mantra is any word or phrase that feels good for you. You can repeat your mantra silently or aloud. It can be an encouragement, a prayer or a sound to soothe and relax. Here are some of my favourites:

Peace

I am safe, I am loved.

Thank You

Sat Nam

Today's Calm Practice: Mantra Meditation

Take ten minutes today to practice mantra meditation. You can choose any mantra - in Sanskrit, English or another language. You can pray in your own faith tradition if you wish. You might like to place your fingers in Gyan Mudra, or use a Mala or Rosary if you have one. You can sit for this meditation, or you could repeat your mantra while out walking.

One lovely way to meditate is to sit with one hand on your heart and the other hand resting in your lap. Close your eyes and quietly repeat 'I am'. Continue for five to ten minutes. Then rest and relax.

DAY TWENTY-SEVEN: YOGA NIDRA

Anxious, tired and stressed people arrive at my Yoga studio desperate for rest. One of my greatest joys as a Yoga teacher is sharing the practice of Yoga Nidra. Yoga Nidra, literally translated as 'yogic sleep', is a safe and easy way to enter the healing space between waking and deep sleep. After a few gentle movements and stretches to settle the body, we lie down comfortably with plenty of cushion and blankets. A soothing aroma of lavender or frankincense wafts through the air. The lights are turned down low. Once everyone is cosy, I begin to speak, reassuring everyone that we are safe here. There is no wrong way to do this. All you have to do is rest here while I take you on a journey deep into relaxation....

An Ancient Practice

Yoga Nidra is an ancient practice, referred to in Indian epic poetry and Medieval Hatha Yoga manuals. It has been developed in modern times by Swami Satyananda and his followers in India as well as by Richard Miller, Rod Stryker, Nirlipta Tuli and Uma Dinsmore-Tuli and others across the world. Yoga Nidra has been researched and developed by western psychologists as well as by traditional gurus. It has been used in the military as a therapy for PTSD. There are many styles of Yoga Nidra and the practice continues to evolve.

Benefits of Yoga Nidra

Yoga Nidra is a guided relaxation and meditation. It slows down brainwaves and enables practitioners easily to enter a space of deep calm and rest. It shares some of the characteristics of hypnotherapy. When you practice Yoga Nidra your nervous system enters the parasympathetic state. Here your body and mind naturally recuperate and your immune system works at its best. Healing happens here.

Yoga Nidra is an excellent way to improve your heart rate variability. This enables you to deal better with with life's stresses, both physical and mental. The practice also releases dopamine in the brain. Dopamine is a neurotransmitter which helps you feel happy and contented. Yoga Nidra has been shown to be effective for the management of chronic pain. It has also been used in the clinical treatment of Post Traumatic Stress Disorder with good results.

Yoga Nidra boosts self-esteem and relieves anxiety. It increases creativity and aids self-discovery. It is also great for exhaustion and depression. Yoga Nidra has so many benefits that it is valuable for everyone. You don't need to be fit or active to practice Yoga Nidra. No bending or stretching is required. You simply have to lie down and close your eyes. This means it is accessible for virtually everyone.

Yoga Nidra has been described as an 'adaptogenic practice'. This means that the practice of Yoga Nidra will adapt itself to meet your current needs. Whether you are looking for better sleep, improved productivity, pain management, relaxation or answers to life's questions, Yoga Nidra can support you.

What Happens During Yoga Nidra?

There are different styles and structures of Yoga Nidra but all follow a similar basic approach. You settle down and close your eyes and a teacher leads you on an inner journey of rest. Once you are lying down and comfortable your teacher will guide you though an initial settling and relaxation. This may include breath awareness, diaphragmatic breathing and setting an intention.

Sankalpa

Yoga Nidra often includes an invitation to seek a *Sank-*

alpa or heartfelt desire. This is a personal wish or resolve. Why are you here? What do you seek from your practice? It is best not to try to force an intention for your practice, but rather see if something arises naturally from your heart. It is fine just to enjoy Yoga Nidra for health and relaxation benefits without being aware of a more specific sankalpa. Or you can practice Yoga Nidra as part of a spiritual journey towards a clear purpose. You might have an intention just for today's practice, or your sankalpa might refer to a deeper, even lifelong goal.

Body Awareness

Yoga Nidra nearly always includes a mental journey around the body, resting your consciousness on each body part in turn. Your teacher will guide you as you focus your awareness on different points on your body. This experience is deeply calming and helps ease you into a dreamlike state.

Breath and Opposites

Then there may be a focus on the natural rhythm of the breath, and usually suggestions to observe pairs of opposite feelings or emotions. You may be invited to imagine heat and cold, happiness and sorrow, heaviness and lightness. This may be followed by more breath awareness.

Guided Visualisation and Silence

Many forms of Yoga Nidra involve some form of guided visualisation or inner awareness. You may be taken on an imaginative journey through mountains, forests or gardens. You may be asked to visualise a series of images. You may be invited to witness the space behind your closed eyes. This is a time for dreamlike visions and deep rest. It can become a journey of self discovery. Relax and observe what arises. Your teacher may leave a period of silence for you to continue your inner exploration and enjoy this profound place of peace.

Return to the Waking World

After revising your sankalpa or heart's desire, your teacher will slowly and gently guide you back to the waking state. You may conclude with a few moments of gratitude for the blessings of the practice. Chanting Om or another mantra is a lovely way to close the practice of Yoga Nidra.

Afterwards

After Yoga Nidra you will probably feel very calm and sleepy. It can take some time to return to full wakefulness. If my students have to travel home after their practice I always give them a snack and make sure they are fully awake so that they can drive home safely. It is wonderful to practice Yoga Nidra before bedtime. You will be able to snuggle down afterwards for an excellent night's sleep.

Today's Calm Practice: Yoga Nidra

See if you can access a Yoga Nidra practice today. The best way to experience Yoga Nidra is with an experienced and qualified teacher. Many classes are available, both online and in person. There is no substitute for a live experience where the teacher can watch over you and guide your inner journey. However you can also enjoy many of the benefits by listening to good recordings.

If you would find a recorded practice, I highly recommend the website of the *Yoga Nidra Network*. Here you can find free recordings, training courses and lots of information about this wonderful practice.

BUILDING CALM INTO YOUR LIFE

DAY TWENTY-EIGHT: SACRED SPACE

Certain places instantly make me feel anxious or relaxed. When I used to work in a very stressful job I would feel my pulse racing with worry as soon as I arrived outside my workplace. But my lovely beach hut at Walton on the Naze is my happy place. The moment I set foot on the sand there my shoulders soften and I start to smile. Every single time.

We are material beings, and our physical surroundings have a big impact on how we feel and behave. We learn to associate familiar places with certain feelings and emotional states. Memories of good or bad times are triggered by remembered sights, smells and spaces. Sometimes this makes us sad, but we can harness this ability to develop positive habits. We all benefit from happy places where we can let go of tension and recuperate from daily life. Creating your own sacred space can help you find calm and connection on a regular basis.

Sacred means Special

The word sacred means set apart for a special purpose. It is often associated with religious worship when we think of things or people being set apart for holy purposes. But you do not have to follow a formal faith to have a sacred space. A sacred space can simply be a space which is special for you. It is a place where you feel safe and where you can care for yourself. You are special, and you deserve special space and time for yourself.

Finding Sacred Space with Others

Many people find shared sacred space with others. This might be at a yoga class, a meditation group or religious worship service. One friend describes the river where she swims regularly with friends as her 'church'. Community and relationships are crucial for our wellbeing. Sharing a special place and activity with others can be life affirming. You can find deep calm when spending time with a close friend or lover. Intimacy is a sacred space.

Sacred Space and Healing

Sacred spaces have been recognised as healing environments since ancient times. In the 5th century BC the Greeks constructed a healing city called Epidaurus. Green space and a temperate climate, flowing spring waters and healing baths and rituals all helped to cure wounded soldiers in a place of holistic tranquility. Japanese tea rituals conducted within beautiful gardens were used to support traumatised Samurai warriors and heal a broken society during the brutal civil wars of the 12th to 14th centuries. In modern times studies have demonstrated that hospital patients who can see trees and green spaces from their beds recover more quickly and need fewer painkillers.

Sacred Space at Home

Many of us seek out holidays and retreats in unspoilt natural environments to recover and heal from the battering of our busy world. This is important, but we also need daily sacred space. You can build calm into your everyday life by creating a sacred space at home for meditation, rest and relaxation. I have a special spot in my garden, unseen from the house, where I like to sit to contemplate, journal and pray. For cold or wet weather I also have a sacred space in a corner of an upstairs room. I love to retreat here. I feel nurtured and safe. You can do this too.

You may also have happy places outside the home. Perhaps you have a favourite walk by a river or in a park. Your local place of worship or yoga studio may be special for you. But it is good to have a calming space in your home because this is always accessible.

Creating Your Sacred Space

If you don't already have a regular space for rest and meditation in your home, why not set one up? You don't need a lot of room. The most important thing is to try to find somewhere quiet where you can be undisturbed, at least sometimes. This might be a corner of a bedroom, a balcony, the garden shed or even the bathroom. Look for somewhere you associate with feeling calm and restful. Ideally it is good to have enough space for a comfortable chair, a shelf or small table, or maybe even a Yoga mat. But all our homes are different, so we must be creative with what we have.

Maybe you have young children or a very crowded house. Try talking to the people you live with about your need for quiet space. Sometimes a simple action like lighting a candle (if you can do this safely) or using an aromatherapy diffuser can signal to yourself and others that this is time for calm.

A Busy Mother

I love the story of Susannah Wesley who was mother to ten children back in the eighteenth century. She struggled with poverty, family illness and a difficult husband. Susannah didn't have a quiet room to retreat to away from the constant demands of her family, but she knew she needed sacred space. Her solution was to pull her apron over her head whenever she wanted to pray. Her children learned not to disturb her at these times - sometimes anyway! Susannah created sacred space from what she had available.

For many of us home is a workplace. This can be because of caring and housework responsibilities or because you now work from home. Since the pandemic arrived lots of people are saying that they miss the psychological transition of commuting between home and work. It is especially important for home-based workers to be able to have down-time away from the mental demands of the job. Making a sacred space at home will give you somewhere to escape to and unwind after that difficult meeting, even if the weather is bad outside.

What to Put in Your Sacred Space

What to put in your sacred space is a very personal choice. Keep here whatever you need for your daily calm practices. This might be a journal and pen, a meditation cushion, a yoga mat, a candle. Maybe you have books or cards you like to read for inspiration. You might like to have your prayer beads handy. If you enjoy incense or aromatherapy oils you can have your burner or diffuser nearby.

Then you may wish to add some objects which are meaningful for you or which have calming sensory appeal. These could include flowers, stones, crystals, spiritual or religious figures or symbols. You might like to add a photograph or painting. You could even draw or write something yourself to place here. I like inspirational quotations which are special for me. You can make your sacred space as simple or as busy as you like. You can enjoy being creative.

Change things round from time to time too. During Lent and periods of cleansing I sometimes add a small bowl of sand to remind me of the value of desert experiences. On other occasions I might burn white sage or palo santo sticks for healing. This is my special space, so I can choose what feels important for me. Refreshing the objects and pictures renews my enthusiasm to spend time here if things have got a bit stale.

Comfort

I like to be comfortable when I am meditating and resting. I have several cushions at hand as well as a couple of lovely soft blankets. Make sure you will be warm enough. Going to your sacred space should feel like a lovely treat. Then you will be more likely to spend time here nurturing yourself.

What to Do in Your Sacred Space

Your sacred space is just for you, so you can do whatever you like here. However it is helpful to have a daily routine for calm, rest and self-nurture. Simply sitting is incredibly powerful. You can choose to listen to music, meditate, practice yoga, write a journal, draw, pray or sleep. Enjoy being here.

Today's Calm Practice: Make a Sacred Space

If you don't already have one, begin today to make a sacred space in your home. Think about where would be a good place, and what you would like to have here. It can be as simple or as elaborate as you choose. This is a beautiful gift you are giving to yourself.

If you already have a sacred space at home, spend some time here today. Maybe you would like to change or add something. Relax and allow inspiration to come to you.

DAY TWENTY-NINE: REFLECTION

My family spent a lot of time together during the Covid 19 lockdown in the spring of 2020. Schools were closed, my husband was working from home, and the world felt unsettled and alarming. Sitting around the dinner table every evening, the six of us shared a reflection that we called 'Best and worst things'.

Each family member in turn thought about their day

and then told the others what had been their best and worst experience. Everyone was honest. Often my best thing was my walk in the woods or a joke shared with one of the children. If someone had had an quarrel with a sibling or parent, that might be their worst thing. Other worst things included frustrations at work, a broken kitchen tap or missing friends. Some revelations were painful. Others made us all laugh. This daily time of reflection and sharing helped us support one another. It helped me understand myself and my family members better.

Daily reflection on our choices and responses is a lovely way to discover inner calm. It is a time-honoured approach to personal reflection and growth.

The Examen

Our 'best and worst things' is a version of the meditation known as the *Examen*. The Examen has its roots in Ignatian spirituality. It is an ancient technique of contemplative reflection on the events and experiences of the day. Practicing the Examen regularly helps me understand how I relate to myself, others, God and the Universe.

There are many variations on the Examen, but the basic idea is always the same. By considering the best and worst aspects of your experience you can discover more about yourself, your needs, your hopes and your deepest joys. It helps you feel grateful for what you have. It highlights things you may wish to do differently next time.

Svadhyaya - The Yogic Practice of Self Study

The Examen comes from a Christian tradition but you do not have to be a Christian to benefit from it. It has many similarities with the Yogic practice known as *Svadhyaya* or self-study. The *Bhagavad Gita* and other ancient texts teach us that Yoga is far more than the physical poses we often think of in the West. Yoga means 'union'. It+ is intended to be a journey toward the unification of the self with one's higher Self and the entire Universe. In Yoga we aim to become the best we can possibly be, in body, mind and spirit. Part of this journey is self-study or Svadhyaya. This includes self-awareness, self-knowledge, self-reflection and self-examination. The Examen is a great tool for practising Svadhyaya.

How to Do The Examen

Begin by making yourself quiet and comfortable. Many people like to light a candle. Take some slow breaths and centre your attention in your heart space.

Become aware that you are part of a wonderful Universe. If you believe in God or a Higher Presence, become aware of that loving Presence with you and in you.

Now begin to review the day you have just lived. Many people practice the Examen in the evening, but if you prefer you can do it in the morning and think about yesterday. Recall the events, actions and emotions of the day. Notice what feelings these memories evoke in your body.

When you are ready, ask yourself these questions:

For what moment today am I most grateful?
For what moment today am I least grateful?

When did I feel most fully alive today?
When did I feel drained of life today?

When was I happiest today?
When was I saddest today?

What was the best thing today?
What was the worst thing today?

When today did I have the greatest sense of belonging?
When did I have the least sense of belonging?

You can reflect on these questions in whatever form makes most sense for you. The aim is to notice, feel and acknowledge your own best and worst moments from the day. Do not seek to praise or blame yourself or others. You are on a lifetime journey of self-discovery. Today is just one small step.

Once you have become aware of your answers to the questions, sit quietly with them. You might like to record your answers in a journal, share them with others, pray or meditate, or simply sit.

When you are ready, blow out the candle. Your Examen is complete.

Sharing the Examen with Others

The Examen is a brilliant spiritual and meditative practice to do alone. It is also a wonderful way to share your life with people close to you. Our family sharing of 'best and worst things' around the dinner table helped bring us closer together. It made us more sensitive to one another's needs. Children love this practice. Listening to your child or teenager's reflections on their day is a great way to communicate with them. They can listen to yours too. You might also like to share the Examen with your partner or a close friend. It is simple, vulnerable and powerful.

Benefits of the Examen

The Examen, practised over time, is life-changing. Many people report increased gratitude, a clearer sense of purpose and better relationships. The practice helps with managing anxiety. It is especially useful if you have big life decisions to make. It is a wonderful tool on the path to self-knowledge. The Examen is one of the best ways I know to find lasting calm.

Today's Calm Practice: The Examen

Try the Examen this evening. Light a candle and reflect on the best and worst moments of your day. Share this with your family, friend or loved one if you like. Or write it down in your journal. Go to bed feeling grateful and calm.

DAY THIRTY: CALM FIRST AID

I arrived home from a family camping trip one Sunday evening. Mountains of bags, tents and equipment filled the hallway of my house. Everything needed unpacking and sorting out, and then I had more work to do getting organised for Monday morning. It was already past 7pm. My heart was racing and the workload seemed overwhelming. I started throwing dirty laundry into the washing machine. I made a cross comment to one of the children about the state of the house. Anger and exhaustion reared their snappy heads.

But then I managed to pause, just for a moment. I noticed that I needed some calm space. I stopped. Instead of starting immediately on all the work I sat down and had something to eat. Then I spent half an hour peacefully watering the garden. I gave myself permission to take time to be calm. After that I felt much better. After my little calm break I still managed to get all the essentials done well before bedtime.

Regular Calm and Calm First Aid

Most of this book is about planning daily calm practices. Regular and reliable calm is essential for our health and wellbeing. It's important to diarise calm space every day, but sometimes we need calm 'first aid' too. Recognising that urgent need for calm is powerful. When we have a lot to do, it's easy to feel we don't have time to stop. But that fifteen minute break usually means the jobs get done faster in the end. And we feel better too.

Recognising your Body's Signals

It helps to learn your own body's signals. When I need calm, I often feel hot and sweaty. Sometimes I get a bit shaky too. I get annoyed by little things that usually don't bother me. The piles of junk in my garage waiting for a journey to the tip are suddenly infuriating. My hands can get itchy, and I find it difficult to focus on the task in hand. I am also much more prone to shout!

Your own warning signs may be different. You might notice your heart racing or you might get a headache. Other parts of your body might hurt or your stomach might clench. Everyone is different. The key is being aware of your own body and knowing yourself. The more you practice doing this, the easier it gets.

Stressful Jobs and Angry Arguments

Our bodies react to our environment in remarkable and sensitive ways. They give us crucial clues about what is really going on. When I worked in a particularly difficult role as a midwife, I realised that I had begun to grind my teeth at night and develop pains in my jaw. This realisation convinced me that the stress was excessive and something needed to change. Shortly after this I begun the process of finding a new job.

I have also discovered that one of the best ways to defuse tension in an argument is to stop and ask: Where do you feel it in your body? This can move the whole discussion onto a completely different and more productive level. Suddenly you are both paying attention to feelings instead of focusing on why you are right. When I realise my opponent has painful feelings like me it is hard to stay really angry with him.

Giving yYourself Permission to Pause

When you realise you need a calm break, take one without delay. However busy you feel, give yourself permission to pause. Stop whatever you are doing, and if you can, try to step physically away from the situation. If you are at work or in a public place, get outside, to a break room or to the toilet if need be. Going outdoors can be a lifeline. If other people are driving you crazy, try to step away from them if possible. They will seem more bearable after a brief calm break.

If you are at home, try going to a quiet room, or out into the garden. Sit down or lie down, or take a gentle walk outside. If you feel very anxious, splashing cold water on your face will activate your parasympathetic nervous system quickly and help you calm down. Focus on your breathing. Simply give yourself the precious gift of a little time and space for yourself. It usually helps to drink some water, and often to eat something too.

Maybe you are too agitated to sit still. Try walking outdoors, or do a simple task that engages you with nature. Tend a plant. Care for a pet. Treat yourself with love and respect. Honour your body by giving it the calm space it needs. Taking a brief calming break will make all the difference to your productivity and peace.

Today's Calm Practice: Paying Attention to your Body

Pay attention to your body today. Remember that you need and deserve calm space. Listening to your body will help you notice when you need calm. How do you feel when you are busy or under pressure? How does your body tell you it needs a break? Notice the signs.

If you feel tension rising, stop. Stop whatever you are doing for five to ten minutes, or a bit longer if you can. Go outdoors if possible and look around you. Just sit quietly, take a walk, or do whatever helps you feel calm. Notice how your body feels different after your calm break. When you feel ready, get on with your tasks. Notice whether you get more done.

If you are lucky enough to have a calm day without needing calm first aid then just sit for five to ten minutes anyway. Spend this time noticing how your body feels.

Become aware of your heartbeat, your breathing, any aches and pains, any tension. Paying loving attention to your body is one of the greatest gifts you can give yourself.

DAY THIRTY-ONE: MAKING TIME FOR CALM

I get up at 5.30 every morning to find calm. My favourite time of the day is the peaceful hour before everyone else in my house is awake. In this golden hour I can write, practice yoga, meditate or go for a swim. By 7am I am rushing around sorting out breakfast, packed lunches, laundry and my plans for clients and teaching. I cope with all these demands much better if I have begun my day with some calm space.

Making time for calm is always a challenge. Calm rarely happens by chance. Many people lead busy lives juggling responsibilities like flaming torches. Calm and self-care are often the first casualties. You need a plan to prioritise calm in your life.

Different Lives, Different Plans

Of course different approaches work for different people. The idea of early rising may fill you with horror. You may be a night owl, active and alert until midnight and beyond. I am pretty much a zombie after about 9pm and always tucked up in bed by 11. Understanding your natural rhythms is the first step towards finding time for calm. Then the demands of your work and family need consideration too. The important thing is finding a plan and structure to ensure that crucial rest and relaxation are not left to chance.

Circadian Rhythms

Your body follows daily cycles known as circadian rhythms. This means you are naturally more alert and active at certain times. Your brain has an internal clock known as the suprachiasmatic nucleus. This is regulated by daylight and darkness and by the magnetic field of the earth. Your body prioritises different functions at different times of the day and night. Sleep and digestion, blood pressure and the immune system are all affected and controlled by circadian rhythms. Disturbed rhythms can have serious impacts on your mental and physical health, contributing to insomnia, depression and many diseases.

Making time for calm and rest on a regular basis is a good way to restore imbalances in your circadian rhythms. Shift work, jet lag, caffeine and the changing of the seasons can all upset your body's natural clock. Prioritising restorative practices such as gentle yoga, meditation and rest on a regular basis will help re-set the cycle.

Choosing your Regular Calm Practices

By following the daily calm practices in this book you have learned lots of different ways to find calm. No one would be able to do all of these every day. I hope you have had a chance to try barefoot walking, legs up the wall, alternate nostril breathing, journaling and more. Some practices will have resonated with you easily and you may already have your favourites. Other suggestions may not work so well for you. Not everyone enjoys outdoor swimming or knitting. We do not all want to bake our own bread or sing on a regular basis. Health, geography or caring responsibilities may limit your current possibilities.

It is wonderful to have a rich variety of calming practices to draw on as the need arises. Once you have tried a range of options, you can plan how to make calm a daily part of your life. This is where the real benefits are reaped. Meditation, yoga, aromatherapy and gardening are all most beneficial when practised regularly. You can choose the activities that work best for you right now.

Life is Always Changing

It is said that the one thing we can be certain of is change. Our lives are always in flux - moving forward, growing and developing. I aim always to follow some calming practices, but the particular ones I choose will vary depending on my circumstances.

During the Covid 19 lockdowns I have found daily journaling and breath exercises particularly helpful in calming my anxiety. Regular walks outdoors are essential for my wellbeing, especially in the warmer months. During the winter I rely more on cold water dips and yoga classes, along with crochet in the dark evenings. Meditation and prayer is something I try to prioritise every day. I love receiving fortnightly or monthly reflexology treatments when I can. My relaxing practices naturally change and adapt over time in accordance with my needs and what is available to me.

Your Life As It Is Now

Think how you can make time for regular calm in your life as it is now. What are the best times in your day to find peace and quiet? Are you a morning person, or do you feel calm and reflective in the evening? When is there a natural break in your daily activities? When do you most feel the need for calm?

Ideally you might come up with two or three little islands of calm in your day. You might identify twenty minutes in the morning you could use for meditation or journaling. Maybe you have a short period at lunch time when you can go outside and breathe or take a short walk. Before bed might be a good time for reflection and a little restorative yoga practice. Be realistic and don't expect too much of yourself. One regular calm space is better than six that never materialise in real life.

If you have young children you may have to be especially creative. Can you prioritise some self-care during your toddler's nap time instead of rushing to ge other tasks done? Perhaps a walk with the pushchair could become a time to enjoy a little nature meditation? Or can you ask for some time for yourself in the evening? It is easy to pour energy into caring responsibilities and forget to care for yourself. Making time and space for calm is crucial for your family's needs as well as your own. They need you to be well, balanced and happy.

Daily, Weekly, Occasional

Some calm practices like journaling or meditation are best practised every day or as often as realistically possible. Eating well, keeping a gratitude journal or using aromatherapy can help you have a good day every day. But you can also plan for weekly and less regular calm spaces in your life. A yoga class every Friday or a massage once a month works well for many people. Retreats, holidays and sound immersion experiences might be occasional treats to boost your self-care. Escapes like these complement and balance the steady, daily nurture of regular calming practice.

Today's Calm Practice: Plan Regular Time for Calm

You need calm, rest and relaxation every day. These are as important for your health and wellbeing as your daily food. Commit now to nurture yourself every day with calming practices you enjoy. You are investing in your future health and happiness.

Sit down quietly today with a notebook and pen. A cup of tea might be nice too. Spend some time thinking about how to plan regular times for calm in your life.

Reflect on which are your favourite calming practices, and which ones fit most readily into your current routines. Write down some ideas about daily and weekly times for calm and restoration. Don't rush this. Listen to your heart and think about what feels right. When you are ready, begin to make a plan. Then start to put it into practice.

THANK YOU FOR JOINING ME FOR THESE THIRTY-ONE DAYS OF CALM.

I hope you have discovered some new calming practices. Maybe you have reawakened some old interests too. If you have been able to find a little more calm and rest in your busy life then I am honoured to have been of service.

Please take from this book whatever seems best for you, and put the rest aside for now. Try to make a few changes to your daily life, however small, which will nurture your wellbeing. Just ten minutes each day is enough to make a difference.

I wish you peace, contentment and calm on your precious life's journey.

   With love,
   Karen xx

LINKS AND FURTHER READING

Calm and The Nervous System

Description of the nervous system: https://en.wikipedia.org/wiki/Nervous_system

Functions of the Vagus Nerve:

https://www.ncbi.nlm.nih.gov/pmc/articles/PMC5859128/

Body Scan

Models and eating disorders

https://www.harpersbazaar.com/culture/features/a21207343/bridget-malcolm-eating-disorder-anxiety/

Walking Barefoot

If you would like to learn more about the health benefits of connection to the earth, there is a fascinating book called "Earthing" by Clint Ober which goes into this in much more detail:

https://www.amazon.co.uk/Earthing-Most-Important-Health-Discovery/dp/1591203740/ref=sr_1_1?

crid=221PVPDKAY792&dchild=1&keywords=earthing&qid=1596606566&sprefix=earthing%2Caps%2C158&sr=8-1

https://www.amacad.org/publication/indigenous-americans-spirituality-and-ecos

http://www.bridgewater.nhs.uk/wp-content/uploads/2012/11/Foot-Facts.pdf

https://www.nhs.uk/conditions/peripheral-neuropathy/

https://www.ncbi.nlm.nih.gov/pmc/articles/PMC3265077/

https://www.painscience.com/articles/barefoot-running.php

Restorative Yoga

https://choosemuse.com/blog/a-deep-dive-into-brainwaves-brainwave-frequencies-explained-2/?utm_source=google&utm_medium=cpc&utm_campaign=ToF_All_Search_Dynamic_Website&utm_term=--b&utm_content=All_Pages--419464376827&gclid=CjwKCAjwsan5BRAOEiwALzomX2TEgBL1emMcoOXHC4JlBhb-Joq1Kiir7dVHLyMgM-xWmhGOdTWPs8BoCEgcQAvD_BwE

https://nhahealth.com/brainwaves-the-language/

Nourishing Food

If you would like to know more about eating well, The British Heart Foundation website has lots of great information about healthy diet. You can read more here:

https://www.bhf.org.uk/informationsupport/heart-matters-magazine/nutrition/ask-the-expert/addicted-to-sugar

Here is some encouraging information about the health benefits of dark chocolate https://www.bbcgoodfood.com/howto/guide/dark-chocolate-good-you

Secure and Loving Touch

https://www.appliedbehavioranalysisedu.org/what-is-deep-pressure-stimulation/

https://www.sciencedirect.com/science/article/pii/S0929664616301735

https://www.topdoctors.co.uk/medical-articles/why-we-touch-our-face-why-it-s-hard-to-stop

https://www.healthline.com/health/anxiety/do-weighted-blankets-work#who-may-benefit

Turning Upside Down

https://www.yogajournal.com/practice/the-importance-of-shoulderstand-and-headstand#:~:text=By%20referring%20to%20Sirsasana%20(Headstand,and%20they%20are%20a%20pair.

https://www.ekhartyoga.com/articles/practice/all-about-yoga-inversions#:~:text=Inversions%20are%20yoga%20poses%20where,benefits%20of%20being%20upside%20down.

https://study.com/academy/lesson/regulation-of-blood-pressure-short-term-regulation-baroreceptors.html#:~:text=monitored%20by%20baroreceptors.-,Baroreceptors%20are%20special%20receptors%20that%20detect%20changes%20in%20your%20blood,increased%20activity%20within%20the%20baroreceptors.

https://www.amazon.co.uk/Iyengar-Holistic-Health-Step-Step/dp/1409343472/ref=sr_1_1_sspa?crid=GA539GZZW0EA&dchild=1&keywords=iyengar+yoga+books&qid=1596962281&sprefix=iyengar%2Caps%2C144&sr=8-1-spons&psc=1&spLa=ZW5jcnlwdGVkUXVhbGlmaWVyPUExNkRMNlk3MDUxRllSJmVuY3J5cHRlZElkPUEwMzU0MzIwMk8wTDRMU1k4RTRTMCZlbmNyeXB0ZWRBZElkPUEwNjI3Mjg4MlAzS0wyV1pGNlIyMCZ3aWRnZXROYW1lPXNwX2F0ZiZhY3Rpb249Y2xpY2tSZWRpcmVjdCZkb05vdExvZ0NsaWNrPXRydWU=

Calming Essential Oils

Aromatherapy is a massive and fascinating subject. There is so much to learn. If you would like to explore further, there are some great books available. You can also take courses. I recommend Neals Yard Remedies as a good place to start to discover oils, books and information. You can see more about their current courses here. https://www.nealsyardremedies.com/course-categories/aromatherapy-courses/

https://www.nhs.uk/conditions/burns-and-scalds/

https://www.healthline.com/health/essential-oil-for-burns

https://www.ncbi.nlm.nih.gov/pmc/articles/PMC4880962/

https://www.degruyter.com/view/journals/znc/46/11-12/article-p1067.xml

https://www.livescience.com/why-smells-trigger-memories.html#:~:text=The%20short%20answer%20is%20that,is%20unique%20among%20your%20senses.

https://www.newdirectionsaromatics.com/blog/products/all-about-frankincense-oil.html

Cool Water

https://www.usgs.gov/special-topic/water-science-school/science/water-you-water-and-human-body?qt-
https://www.wimhofmethod.com/science_center_objects=0#qt-science_center_objectshttps://www.ncbi.nlm.nih.gov/books/NBK538245/

https://meassociation.org.uk/wp-content/uploads/MEA-Summary-Review-Dysfunctional-ANS-in-MECFS-24.01.18.pdf

https://pdfs.semanticscholar.org/f3d0/1ae0f7643cf20bac5f959d469103d3f1af46.pdf

https://www.outdoorswimmingsociety.com/category/survive/getting-started/

Breath Awareness

https://carta.anthropogeny.org/libraries/bibliography/evolution-human-speech-role-enhanced-breathing-control

https://liveanddare.com/history-of-meditation

https://d1wqtxts1xzle7.cloudfront.net/47860048/j.jbmt.2005.09.00320160807-16752-1g4bkai.pdf?1470577665=&response-content-disposition=inline%3B+filename%3DBreath_therapy_for_chronic_low_back_pain.pdf&Expires=1597220473&Signature=QJlUi2T2oGKCsjTSH5TPM8dhnfm57N2~KKAP5XF1NpwFOUDcLQbKlW7mWY4oKtdhFjJNheJQjrwe6di0ZvgZyrz87RBWudWKV9cvawrPDNqi1dZjpGSQX-cWW2fFIOEkwNUDYWzrmYjTaGLeYyxWcB7k41CCsfxD-

zaM7ZqKcHGcLm2LJ5uk~emEcEUKB2u3O4cJ0p5nV9WAOd-WiKneTXS~wUMxnVfxUCygO11Q6-v~zuRnKwoojN3I2D48yDkvC3xMhd87TypIQStl6XmUDScr-9BMpO-LTwUdYCepF2Z6mLMgOAXLyGATd0vxjI8FBZ7L-9-y90xS4BgN6HfBZmIOg__&Key-Pair-Id=APKAJLOHF5GGSLRBV4ZA

https://thecalmspace.co.uk/2020/08/02/finding-your-calm-space-calm-and-the-nervous-system/

Belly Breathing

https://www.healthline.com/health/diaphragmatic-breathing

https://www.nqa.org/index.php?option=com_dailyplanetblog&view=entry&year=2019&month=07&day=01&id=35:research-on-diaphragmatic-breathing#:~:text=Diaphragmatic%20breathing%20activates%20your%20parasympathetic,to%20slow%20down%20and%20heal.

https://www.healthline.com/human-body-maps/diaphragm

https://yogamedicine.com/power-diaphragm-part/#:~:text=It%20sends%20signals%20out%20from,we%20get%20as%20an%20effect.

Alternate Nostril Breathing

https://www.yogajournal.com/poses/channel-cleaning-breath

https://www.yogajournal.com/yoga-101/balancing-act-2

http://www.medicaldiscoverynews.com/shows/616-nose.html

https://www.ncbi.nlm.nih.gov/pmc/articles/PMC5053491/#:~:text=One%20such%20large%2Dscale%20cycle,right

%20over%20time%20%5B2%5D.
https://sequencewiz.org/2014/08/06/one-nostril-breathing/

Chanting and Singing

https://thesingersworkshop.com/breath-control/#:~:text=Breathing%20is%20the%20single%20most,for%20the%20sound%20you%20want.&text=How%20you%20exhale%20controls%20the,the%20pitch%20and%20the%20tone.

http://black-mary.com/8-reasons-why-yoga-can-be-good-for-your-voice/

https://www.singupfoundation.org/singing-health?gclid=CjwKCAjwj975BRBUEiwA4whRBzKBsDpUS9PA5swc8EVX4WRco7VzUqYc8AZ2bGV62eacZ4c9nqUpx-RoCW6MQAvD_BwE

https://www.ekhartyoga.com/articles/practice/an-introduction-to-kirtan-the-songs-of-yoga

https://www.yogajournal.com/yoga-101/mastering-om

https://www.livescience.com/4897-earth-hum-sounds-mysterious.html

If you would like to listen to Kirtan and join in at home, I highly recommend David Lurey who leads Kirtan on the Ekhart Yoga website. He also has some lovely recordings which you can find on Spotify or Apple Music.
https://www.ekhartyoga.com/teachers/david-lurey

Walking Outdoors

https://www.ncbi.nlm.nih.gov/pmc/articles/PMC4377926/

https://blog.frontiersin.org/2018/06/07/neuroscience-leg-exercise-brain-nervous-system-health/

https://www.nationalgeographic.com/magazine/2016/01/call-to-wild/

https://www.forestryengland.uk/blog/forest-bathing

Nature Meditation

https://www.yogajournal.com/meditation/natural-wonder

https://www.theyogasanctuary.biz/exploring-patanjalis-yoga-sutras-sutra-1-2/

https://io9.gizmodo.com/15-uncanny-examples-of-the-golden-ratio-in-nature-5985588

Engaging with Nature

https://www.mind.org.uk/information-support/tips-for-everyday-living/nature-and-mental-health/how-nature-benefits-mental-health/

https://www.kew.org/read-and-watch/windowsill-veg-herbs

https://blog.parkrun.com/uk/
https://www.borrowmydoggy.com/

https://www.rspb.org.uk/birds-and-wildlife/

https://www.wildlifetrusts.org/closer-to-nature/volunteer

https://www.beachclean.net/
https://www.farmgarden.org.uk/

https://skyandtelescope.org/astronomy-resources/stargazing-basics/how-to-start-right-in-astronomy/

Listening Meditation

https://nexus.jefferson.edu/science-and-technology/how-tomanipulate-brain-waves-for-a-better-mental-state/

https://brainworksneurotherapy.com/types-brainwave-entrainment

https://www.ncbi.nlm.nih.gov/pmc/articles/PMC6130927/

https://www.mindlikewaterwellbeing.com/ayurvedic-sound-massage

Baking Bread

https://www.bbc.co.uk/food/recipes/paul_hollywoods_crusty_83536

https://www.irishfoodguide.ie/2015/09/october-24th-is-international-bake.html#:~:text=%22Bake%20Bread%20For%20Peace%20has,the%20world%20they%20live%20in.%22

https://www.myjewishlearning.com/article/hamotzi-the-deeper-significance-of-the-blessing-over-bread/

Journaling

https://thedoctorweighsin.com/can-journaling-improve-your-mental-health/

https://www.tinyhabits.com/welcome

https://jamesclear.com/habit-triggers

https://zapier.com/blog/best-journaling-apps/

https://www.amazon.co.uk/Artists-Way-Discovering-Recovering-Creative/dp/1509829474/ref=sr_1_1?adgrpid=56854771407&dchild=1&gclid=Cj0KCQjwhIP6BRC-MARIsALu9Lfl63Md_tdj5ZaHoTxSCu79LMs8vG-caAOcqy2YowTEtfdmrdrAWMP8aAnZVEALw_wcB&hvadid=259067773136&hvdev=c&hvlocphy=9044870&hvnetw=g&hvqmt=e&hvrand=6554704003137665269&hvtargid=kwd-297

816099778&hydadcr=28151_1724832&keywords=the+artist%27s+way&qid=1598089699&sr=8-1&tag=googhydr-21

Crafting and Creativity

https://www.independent.co.uk/life-style/knitting-reduces-anxiety-depression-chronic-pain-slows-dementia-research-knit-for-peace-uk-a8254341.html

https://www.psychologytoday.com/gb/articles/199707/finding-flow
https://knitforpeace.org.uk/

Haiku

https://kripalu.org/resources/art-haiku-clear-eyes-clear-mind

https://www.readpoetry.com/10-vivid-haikus-to-leave-you-breathless/

Gratitude

https://www.happierhuman.com/benefits-of-gratitude/

https://www.weforum.org/agenda/2017/07/you-are-naturally-biased-to-negative/

https://www.amazon.co.uk/One-Thousand-Gifts-Fully-Right/dp/0310321913/ref=sr_1_1?adgrpid=48770925250&dchild=1&gclid=CjwKCAjwmf_4BRABEiwAGhDfScGZYUcTgai2bVkDJcGABR6wbjHKUU7eWp9_TkJo4GumrmtFbaYPxoChnYQAvD_BwE&hvadid=259043516541&hvdev=c&hvlocphy=1007115&hvnetw=g&hvqmt=b&hvrand=6758437453133664918&hvtargid=kwd-325770669034&hydadcr=24458_1816148&keywords=ann+voskamp+one+thousand

+gifts&qid=1595950294&sr=8-1&tag=googhydr-21

Loving Kindness

People and Organisations for Help When Relationships Get Difficult:

https://www.relate.org.uk/

https://www.nationaldahelpline.org.uk/

https://www.nhs.uk/conditions/counselling/

https://news.sky.com/story/mother-of-murdered-nhs-worker-forgives-his-killers-11980881

https://www.psychologytoday.com/gb/blog/the-addiction-connection/201409/the-psychology-forgiveness

https://www.apa.org/monitor/2017/01/ce-corner

https://sophiemessager.com/free-yourself-from-trauma/

https://www.hypnotherapy-directory.org.uk/memberarticles/does-hypnosis-work-for-anger-management

https://thebuddhistcentre.com/text/loving-kindness-meditation

Mantra Meditation

https://www.yogajournal.com/yoga-101/types-of-yoga/kundalini

https://www.shambhala.com/snowlion_articles/om-mani-padme-hum-dalai-lama/

https://www.yogajournal.com/yoga-101/mantras-101-the-science-behind-finding-your-mantra-and-how-to-practice-it

https://understandquran.com/for-when-the-going-gets-tough-5-powerful-muslim-mantras-from-the-quran-cc/

https://www.orthodoxprayer.org/Jesus%20Prayer.html

https://www.malaprayer.com/blogs/news/everything-you-need-to-know-about-mala-prayer-necklaces

https://culturetaste.com/blog/31_prayer-beads-worldwide-a-brief-history.html

https://fitsri.com/yoga/gyan-mudra#:~:text=Meaning%20of%20Gyan%20Mudra,one's%20knowledge%20and%20excites%20wisdom.&text=Other%20names%20of%20Gyan%20mudra,Jnana%20mudra%20and%20Chin%20mudra.
https://www.runnersblueprint.com/running-mantras/

Yoga Nidra

https://www.ekhartyoga.com/resources/styles/yoga-nidra#:~:text=Yoga%20Nidra%20is%20an%20ancient,1000%20BC%20through%20verbal%20teaching).&text=Yoga%20Nidra%20continues%20to%20evolve.

https://en.wikipedia.org/wiki/Yoga_nidra
https://www.yoganidranetwork.org/

https://www.liebertpub.com/doi/10.1089/acm.2011.0331

https://www.sciencedirect.com/science/article/abs/pii/S0926641001001069?via%3Dihub

https://apps.dtic.mil/dtic/tr/fulltext/u2/a523510.pdf

https://www.sciencedirect.com/science/article/abs/pii/S1744388118308089?via%3Dihub

Sacred Space

https://glosbe.com/en/en/set%20apart%20as%20sacred

http://apm.amegroups.com/article/view/15559/15655

https://sustainablehealthcare.org.uk/what-we-do/green-space-and-health#:~:text=Natural%20environments%20have%20enormous%20benefits,see%20trees%20from%20their%20beds.

https://www.martineoborne.com/susanna-wesleys-apron-and-other-places-to-pray/

Self Awareness and the Examen

If you would like to learn more about the Examen, I highly recommend the beautifully illustrated book, *Sleeping with Bread - Holding What Gives You Life* by Dennis, Sheila and Matthew Linn.

https://www.amazon.co.uk/Sleeping-Bread-Holding-What-Gives/dp/0809135795#:~:text=Taken%20from%20the%20spiritual%20exercises,one%20in%20the%20right%20direction

https://www.ignatianspirituality.com/ignatian-prayer/the-examen/

https://www.pathwaystogod.org/my-prayer-life/examen

https://www.calmwithyoga.com/how-to-practice-svadhyaya-the-yogic-principle-of-self-study/

Building Calm into Your Life

https://www.sleepfoundation.org/articles/what-circadian-rhythm

ABOUT THE AUTHOR

Karen Lawrence

Karen Lawrence is a Yoga teacher, Reflexologist and Mum of seven. She previously worked as a midwife and health visitor. Karen's quest for calm began when she was overwhelmed by the pressures of her caring responsibilities. She has discovered the remarkable health and wellbeing benefits of slow yoga, meditation, spending time in nature, gratitude practices and more.

When she is not teaching, writing or caring for her family, Karen loves open water swimming and hiking long trails with her husband. She is one of those crazy people who likes to dip in icy lakes and rivers though the winter.

You can learn more about Karen's Yoga classes and therapies at her Yoga Business website:

https://thecalmspace.co.uk/

You can read more of Karen's writing at her Author and Blogger website:
https://karenlawrenceauthor.com/

Printed in Great Britain
by Amazon